BOOK
OF
TRUTHS
Thompson Truths
— VOLUME I —

McDougal & Associates

BOOK

OF

TRUTHS

Thompson Truths

— VOLUME I —

Benton T. Thompson, III

Published by:

McDougal & Associates
18896 Greenwell Springs Road
Greenwell Springs, LA 70739
www.thepublishedword.com

ISBN 978-1-950398-74-4

Printed on demand in the U.S., the U.K., Australia, and the UAE.
For Worldwide Distribution

Books by
Benton T. Thompson, III

Contents

Introduction

Why **Thompson Truths**? A Thompson Truth is an homage to my father, the late great Reverend Benton T. Thompson Jr., and the wisdom nuggets he shared with all those whom he loved. For years I would often share the insights I received from him with others, until many have commented that they felt like my father was their father too. They were so glad I had shared with them the wisdom he shared with his family concerning everyday living.

My dad was wonderful, and he always desired to help anyone he could. He was a teacher at heart. To that end, Thompson Truths share wisdom and insights about life lessons, something we all need.

What is a **Thompson Truth**? It is a reminder of just how much God loves and cares for us. Sometimes, amidst the difficulties or unknowns of life, it can be easy to forget about God's true purpose for our life. He always wants us to know that we are never alone. The Bible compares God to a hen always hovering over her chicks. It can be very comforting to know that God is always there, watching, waiting for an opportunity to help us, His chicks, His children.

God's words manifest His presence in our lives, and when we recount His words, He shows up. This can be very reassuring when we feel beat down by responsibilities. That's why I wanted to share with you these 44 timeless truths which contain Gods promises and wisdom from His Word, as a personal resource that we can all draw strength from, no matter where we are in our spiritual walk.

Some call these PRPs, Practical, Relatable Parables. This book features encouraging, practical, and relatable hope-filled devotionals about God's love, self-love, healing, guidance, community, and relationships. They will be by your side anytime you need some confident assurance of God's great love for you.

I believe that, through these Thompson Truth devotionals, you will be reinvigorated and inspired, and will remain confident of God's goodness toward you in every area of your life. I hope you get to know God's truths personally for your life through this *Book of Truths*.

Benton T. Thompson, III

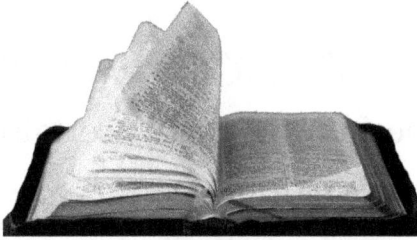

Living Looking Back

If we keep living looking back, all we are going to get is a stiff neck, and then we won't be able to turn around and see what God has for us coming our way. I've heard it said that we should only allow our past to serve as a propeller on our life ship, to thrust us toward our new land. We must be mindful not to live in the past, for doing so can prove to be harmful, even dangerous at times.

What do I mean by living in the past? When we constantly refer to how things "used to be," that's living in the past. Remembering the past is certainly not a sin, but constantly desiring to return to it could be. When we insist on reliving again and again the experiences of the past, we delay the coming glory of the new day ahead.

There is an allegory that tells the story of how a man, his wife, and their two daughters were living in an unhealthy environment for their family. Although they were in a toxic situation, they continued to stay year after year. They kept repeating the same old cycle over and over again.

Wash! Rinse! Repeat!

Wash! Rinse! Repeat!

Finally, one day, something happened that was so horrific they had to leave.

They were being forced out. Sometimes, however, we may leave a situation with our head but not with our heart. This was the case for the man's wife. As they were leaving, she kept remembering how things used to be.

Sometimes we get convenient amnesia. We only remember the good, not the bad. She relived the past so often that she actually stopped moving forward. Then, she gave in to the temptation and decided to turn around and head back, back to the drama, back to the pain, back to what had already been put behind her.

You know how we do. Sometimes we think it's easier to go back than it is to go forward. Or so we think, until we find out that it isn't.

Which reminds me of another saying I heard: "There are those who prefer a known slavery rather than an unknown freedom." Sometimes there's a familiar security in the limitations we've known.

When the wife turned around to head back, she became a huge pile of salt. Yes, salt ... hard, unchanging, and unaffected by some obvious deterrents. That salt represented the condition of her heart. She had become salty, petty, and bitter.

The moral of the story is this: if we get stuck living looking back into our past, then we'll never get to what's waiting for us up ahead—that new thing!

Meanwhile, the woman's husband, Lot, and their two daughters went on to see the new land and new things God had for them.

Living life is like driving a car. You must go forward to advance, to get to your destiny/destination. Someone might say, "But you can also look behind you in a car." This is true ...when you look through a five- inch-wide and three-inch tall, tiny, rear-view mirror. Or you could look at the big picture through the five-foot-wide and two-foot-high windshield. Notice the disparity in size: five feet vs. five inches.

A rearview mirror is only made to see a small portion of what is behind you. It was never designed for you to see all that is behind. A windshield is designed to give you a full view of all that is before you. Your future is much bigger than your past.

Continuing to live in your yesterday robs you of the joys of today and tomorrow. Look at life through the windshield of hope, hope for a better new day ahead!

This is a Thompson Truth!

NOW, WRITE YOUR TRUTH:

_____

_____

_____

_____

_____

_____

_____

_____

_____

_____

_____

_____

_____

_____

_____

_____

_____

Athazagoraphobia

For all those who might be wondering if this is just some made-up word, YES, it is. But I didn't make it up. It's in the dictionary. Look it up for yourself.

Recently, on one of my podcasts, we had a talk about the ever-popular board game called Scrabble. Feel free to review that podcast again, if you like, or listen for the first time, if you haven't yet.[1]

_____

1. I encourage you to visit my site:
   www.bentonthompsoniii.com/thompsontruths

Today's word would be great for Scrabble. You could get a lot of points using it. However, this talk is not about Scrabble; it's about how we can feel sometimes.

Let's break athazagoraphobia down to see what it means. *Phobia*, as we know, is fear. *Agora* refers to a place, and *athaz* deals with the actions of someone. Hence *athazagoraphobia* is "a fear that someone will leave us somewhere." If the word were used in reference to our faith, we would be afraid that God would leave us. What a terrifying thought! None of us wants to feel forgotten, right?

Whether waiting as a child left at school or home, waiting as an adult for a ride, or waiting for someone to keep their word about a promise they made, no one wants to feel forgotten, certainly not by God. No one wants to be left waiting.

The real root issue here is the waiting. When we are made to wait, we become afraid that we might be left and forgotten about. "God," we might pray, "I don't want to wait. You might forget about me. You might forget what You told me or what You promised me. Lord, please don't make me wait. I don't like waiting!"

Amen or oh, me? For many of us, waiting can seem long, discouraging, and challenging. It can conjure up images of bad things coming to those who wait. That's because we see waiting as inactivity ... except for the biting of our nails part. We see waiting as watching the calendar or clock while we wait for the other shoe or an anvil to drop on our heads and crush us. That's the only active part we know about while waiting.

But God sees waiting as an opportunity for us to grow stronger while we wait. Look at this revelation that God gave to His prophet Isaiah.

"Those who wait on the LORD shall renew their strength; they will be able to soar like an eagle, they shall run and not get tired, they shall walk and not faint."

In God's version of waiting, we gain strength and stamina and are elevated. Biting our nails, pacing the floor, staying up late and getting sick with worry, checking the mail, or calling folks repeatedly will not produce these kind of results. Obviously, our type of waiting differs greatly from God's type of waiting.

Maybe that was just a onetime deal. Let's see if we can find another example. As Abraham was waiting (on God's promise of a child), he grew in strength. God's waiting must resemble a workout. That's why folks are getting stronger.

How can we get stronger like Isaiah and Abraham did while waiting on God? Like so many other things, there are Do's and Don'ts involved with the process. I would like to share three of each for us to focus on.

Here are the Don'ts:

- Don't grumble while you're waiting.
- Don't give up while you're waiting.
- Don't go hide while you're waiting.

If we do any of these, then we'll miss the great blessing God has been preparing for us.

Now, let's check out the Do's:

- Read while you are waiting. Get to know God better by reading His Word.
- Reflect while you are waiting. Reflect on all the blessings God has given us.
- Relief while you are waiting. Be a blessing to someone else who is in need.

Use your time of waiting to become a better student of God's Word and His ways. Use your time of waiting to learn that God is the best time manager there is. He will do everything for us at the exact best moment in time. Nothing is wasted, nothing has been forgotten, and everything will be attended to.

Therefore, we don't have to be afraid of waiting on God and His timing. All things will be better for us because we have learned to wait God's way.

God has promised that He would never leave us or forget about us. So, we don't have to worry about that part with Him. Therefore, let's use our time of waiting to get stronger in our faith and trust in God.

Waiting is not about what we can or will get done once the time of waiting is over; waiting it is about how strong we can become in our faith as a result of our "Wait Training." It's time to get buffed in the Spirit!

This is a Thompson Truth

NOW, WRITE YOUR TRUTH:

_____

_____

_____

_____

_____

_____

_____

_____

_____

_____

_____

_____

_____

_____

_____

_____

Being Waitlisted

These days we're being handed pagers or buzzers and are expected to watch screens and boards for updates, to talk to robots, and are being asked by robots if we are robots. After that, if you're lucky, you might get put in a que and thus told that you are not the priority. There are at least 215 people more important than you. You're number 216. However, if you don't want to wait, we can call you back in anywhere from 137 minutes to 6 days.

It seems like everywhere you turn these days someone has some sort of a waitlist they are putting you on. If you call a business, quite often they will waitlist you before even addressing your call.

When you go out to eat at a nice restaurant, they could easily say there will be a two-hour wait. Even if you just want something quick and easy, like take-out food, you still have to get in line and get put on hold or waitlisted. The doctor, dentist, hospital, DMV, airports, grocery stores, retail stores, and theaters, all make you wait. You mean to tell me I can't even use the restroom or have fun without waiting in a line? Yep!

Am I the only one who feels that sometimes even our prayers get waitlisted?

When I first came to know about God, it seemed like my prayers were being answered immediately. By the time I finished praying, He had already done it. Then, as time went on, it seemed like I was waiting longer and longer for my prayers to be answered. Perhaps you can identify with this too?

What had previously taken a few minutes was now taking years to complete. Minutes turned to days, days turned to months, and months turned to decades, and it seemed to take longer and longer to get an answer. Sometimes there was no answer at all. It felt like being waitlisted all over again.

One possibility for the wait might be that the complexity of the prayers has increased.

When we were new to this, it was, "Lord, please just give me an opportunity to tell someone how good You are." Then it became, "Lord, I need three cars, a house, and a mate by the end of next week."

This reminds me of my grandmother's cooking. She could prepare a sandwich relatively quickly, but a full meal was a completely different story. She had to wash the green beans thoroughly before she meticulously snapped each of them, one by one. Don't even think about mentioning canned goods to her!

Then she had to get out all the ingredients to make the corn bread. Eggs had to be cracked, fresh cornmeal, butter, sugar, and salt all had to be on hand and then mixed together to perfection.

Then, of course, the chicken had to be washed, cleaned, cut up, and seasoned long before she could fry it in a pan to a golden crisp. Potatoes had to be peeled, and so on, and so on. A lot goes into a personalized home-cooked meal.

Everything good takes a while to prepare, and maybe it's the same way with God. His Word says, *"No good thing will I hold back from those who love me."* This tells me that God cooks only the good "stuff" for us. So, it's going to take a little longer.

In the Old Testament, God cooked almost everyone's blessings slow and thorough, just like my grandmother. There are some references to wait or waiting mentioned in twenty-six of the thirty-nine books in the Old Testament, and thirteen out of the twenty-seven books in the New Testament. This means that all twelve of the tribes of Israel, Joshua, Samuel, Hosea, Micah, Habakkuk, Zephaniah, David, Abraham, Nehemiah, Job, Elijah, Isaiah, Ezra, Zechariah, Daniel, Jesus, His disciples, and countless other believers all had to wait on God to do His thing. Odds are pretty good that we're going to have to wait too.

You might have noticed that there are a lot of spiritual giants on the wait list. Let's look at how a few of them handled being waitlisted:

Elijah wanted to show everyone that God would send down fire from Heaven to burn water, so he prayed while being waitlisted (see 1 Kings 18).

Paul was wrongly imprisoned and looked for God to deliver him. He and Silas sang while they were being waitlisted (see Acts 16).

Daniel prayed and got no answer at all and wondered why he had been waitlisted. Some of us are right there with Brother Daniel, waiting and wondering.

Sometimes, like Daniel, we, too, must wait for reinforcements to come. Why? Because the enemy has seen our future long before we did (see Daniel 10).

God placed Habakkuk as a watchman over a whole nation. Yet he, too, was waitlisted. Despite the delay, he waited with expectancy for God (see Habakkuk 1).

Let's review: One prayed, one praised, one got no answer at all initially, but, like Habakkuk, they all waited with an expectant heart.

Waiting is a position, just like standing, kneeling, and running are positions. We stand with our legs locked in position, to be upright in order to see God's glory. We kneel with legs bent, as we prepare to lie prostrate before the Almighty. We run with our legs moving like we are stomping with praise for the things that God has already done for us. And we wait with a heart of expectancy, believing that soon we shall reap if we faint not.

If you've prayed and asked God for answers but find yourself waiting longer than you expected, take a moment now to thank Him in advance for His answer. Trust that He is working everything out behind the scenes on your behalf. Don't give up, but look up, with hope and expectancy, believing to see Him respond. Remember, no good thing will He withhold from those who love Him.

Lord, we thank You for remaining faithful to us. Help us to have hope and expectancy as we wait for Your answers to our prayers.

In Jesus' name.

Amen!

This is a Thompson Truth!

NOW, WRITE YOUR TRUTH:

_____

_____

_____

_____

_____

_____

_____

_____

_____

_____

_____

_____

_____

_____

_____

_____

_____

_____

4

Is God Stressing You?

Is God stressing you? Does it seem like He's not getting you out of a stressful situation you're in? Is He just allowing you to sit in your stress? Great! What do I mean by that? Please allow me to explain myself.

For most of us, when we think of stress, we automatically associate it with negativity. Too much is required of us, there's not enough time or resources, the lift is too heavy, the goal is not worth the effort, there is unfair treatment, I'm being targeted, or someone has unreasonable expectations of me. "I can't do this!" "Why me?" These are common thoughts that lead to stress. Stress is our reaction to physical, emotional, and intellectual changes or challenges. However, the truth is that stress can differ from person to person. What might be stressful for one could be a breeze for another. Hence, stress is not the big bad boogy man we think it is.

Stress is seen as negative because we view the situation or circumstance as negative. Let me say that again. We view stress as something negative because we feel the situation we're in is negative/wrong/unfair/too much/more than we can bear. Thus we think negative thoughts about what we deem to be a negative situation or circumstance.

What if I told you that there is good stress or a good purpose behind being stressed? Yes, it's called *eustress,* and it means a stress that produces benefits.

Stress can boost your performance and increase your alertness. Stressing causes stretching, and when we stretch, we grow. God places us in eustress, stressful situations, to benefit us.

Many times, we want God to improve our situation, but He wants to improve us in our situation, so that we will be prepared for any situation, now or in the future.

Some like to say, "I'm too blessed to be stressed," but God says we are blessed *because* we are stressed. Blessed by the stress is more like it. Look at what David realized from one of the many stressful situations he found himself in:

"You have enlarged me and caused me to grow when I was in stress/distress; you had mercy on me and heard my prayer" (Psalm 4:1). David saw how he had grown in his faith in God when he was in stress/distress, and he learned to benefit from stress by exercising his faith when he faced stress.

The word *enlarge* means "to make bigger." David was saying, "Lord, You have made me bigger. Lord, You made me grow up in some areas of my life by allowing me to go through what I went through." Many of us might have that same testimony.

It was David who also said, *"Though I travel through death's valley, I will not fear. Because You, O Lord, are the shepherd that leads and guides me through it all."* He saw the benefits in his stress. God's promise is: *"All things work together for my good."*

Jabez was another person who asked God to enlarge him. *"Oh, that You would bless me and enlarge my territory! Let Your hand be with me, and keep me from harm so that I will be free from pain"* (1 Chronicles 4:10). Many have thought that when Jabez asked for an enlarged territory he was only speaking of land and resources. In other words, that he just wanted more "stuff." But then why did he reference his person, his body, his fears? It was more than land. He was referring to his character. *"Grow me up, O Lord, so that I can be ready for the blessing when You send it to me. Please let Your hand be with me. I don't need to get ready; I want to be ready, O Lord, for my blessing. Stress me, O Lord. Stretch me, O Lord, that I may be big enough for my blessing."*

Our lives must be stretched to fit God's plan for us. He is a big God with big plans, so we must develop traits like a rubber band. A rubber band's greatest worth is seen only after it is stretched. God stretches us to make us more useful in the Kingdom of Heaven.

Stretching means trusting. Sometimes it's painful and scary. It creates tension.

But stress and tension are what create balance. They hold everything together in their proper place. Some things would be moving all over the place if not for the stress and tension that hold them in place.

The noun *tension* has its Latin roots in *tendere*, which means "to stretch." A rubber band isn't much use unless it is stretched, and we can only achieve our full potential when we allow God to stretch us to our limits.

Stretching means trusting and reaching out to God instead of letting go and quitting. We must think of ourselves as trapeze artists. Swing out and then stretch to catch God's hand as we fly through the air by faith. We have to stretch to catch the next opportunity God has for us.

We must be willing to come out of our comfort zones and risk being blessed. Yes, I said WE. I'm scared right now, even as I'm writing these words. I know I have a few immediate jumps to make in my life. I can either jump ship or jump out to reach for God's unchanging hand.

I know He won't let me fall. He can't. But that still doesn't mean that I'm not afraid. Maybe that's why we see Him telling folks all the time, *"Fear not!"* He's trying to assure us that He will never let go, and we won't fall. Instead, we'll grow.

Stretching is good for us. It's good to be stretched in all aspects of life. When we stretch a muscle, we get stronger. When we stretch our bodies, we become more flexible. When we stretch our minds, we grow in knowledge. The same can be said for us spiritually. When we stretch our faith, we see God do things we find hard to believe.

If you ever want to see a hard-to-believe blessing, just pray, "Lord, stretch me!" God will always stretch us to do more, not only for His Kingdom, but for ourselves as well!

This is a Thompson Truth!

NOW, WRITE YOUR TRUTH:

_____

_____

_____

_____

_____

_____

_____

_____

_____

_____

_____

_____

_____

_____

_____

5

A New Day

Some of us start the day by hitting the snooze button on the alarm clock, then jumping out of the bed at the last minute, rushing to get ready, and running out the door. Others of us might wake up early in the morning with the mindset that the early bird gets the benefits of the day. We are going to be the first ones there, and we will make sure to get that worm.

But when does a new day actually begin? Scientist tell us that the first moment after the Earth completes one rotation around its axis, a new day begins. A day is typically defined by a twenty-four-hour period. Hence, we consider one minute after midnight the start of a new day.

Days, as a measurement of time, have been around since the very beginning of time. During Creation, something new and different was formed each and every day.

Day One, I would imagine, with all the greatness and grandeur of light appearing for the very first time, was quite spectacular to behold. Instantly everything was made brighter and better by this single event.

On Day Two, the sky was created, which was also equally great. Seeing the blue hues painted across the backdrop of the horizon, with pops of billowy, soft clouds scattered here and there, must have been wonderful.

As creation progressed, day after day, something new and exciting appeared out of nowhere, a new start for each new day. Let's examine how the creation of a new day really began.

In each occurrence, at the conclusion of all the wondrous events that went into making a new day, there was a common statement of fact: *"And the evening and the morning were the first day." "And the evening and the morning were the second day." "And the evening and the morning were the third day."* This statement was repeated over and over again from day one all the way through day six.

During each night, things were also being transformed. The situation was changing. Why do we get night terrors or have nightmares? This tells me that during the darkest hours of the day something new and wonderful is being created for us.

Perhaps you've had a long day. Maybe you would even say it was a bad day. And now it's dark. Well, right in the middle of your darkest hour God is creating something new and better for you.

The sun is preparing itself to shine on you again. You're getting a new sky, with new heights to soar in. Every creature will receive a fresh touch to begin a new day.

Darkness will give birth to light, not just

more darkness as we sometimes feel. At the darkest time of your day, God gives you a new day, a new start, with a new outlook. Take advantage of your new day!

"And the evening and the morning were a new day!"

This is a Thompson Truth!

NOW, WRITE YOUR TRUTH:

_____

_____

_____

_____

_____

_____

_____

_____

_____

_____

_____

_____

_____

_____

_____

_____

6

The Right Ingredients

It is very important to have the right ingredients to make the thing you desire. Whether in cooking or in life, content matters.

Ingredients are the substances you use to combine with one another as you are preparing to make a particular thing that you desire. For example, if you desire some banana bread, you must have bananas as an ingredient to achieve what you want. Or, if you are desiring an apple pie, then it certainly stands to reason that you will definitely need some apples as an ingredient.

God knew the importance of having the right ingredients when He was making things back in the beginning. He desired light, so He made light, but what did He make it from? If you or I desired to make light, what ingredients would we choose to use? Surprisingly, God chose darkness as His ingredient to make light. So, maybe we shouldn't be so afraid of darkness. The light that God created that day wasn't from the sun. The sun was not created until three days later.

To make the plants, trees, and flowers, God used the soil of the earth as an ingredient. That's probably something we might have thought of as well. But, to make fish, sharks, and whales, He used water from the ocean. I certainly didn't see that one coming.

One of God's greatest creations was man, and the ingredient He chose to use to make man from was spirit. God took His own Spirit and His Son's Spirit and blew them into the soul of man. This was done to forge a lasting relationship/connection.

This got me to thinking about the ingredients I've chosen to use in past relationships. I used sight, smell, feelings, touch, knowledge, perception, and the word of others, but I never used spirit to build a lasting relationship.

Again, it is very important to have the right ingredients to make the thing you desire. Maybe I didn't get what I wanted because I didn't use the right ingredients. Hmmm!

This is a Thompson Truth!

NOW, WRITE YOUR TRUTH:

_____

_____

_____

_____

_____

_____

_____

_____

_____

_____

_____

_____

_____

_____

_____

_____

_____

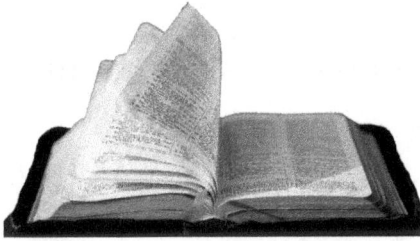

7

The Voice of God

Life is a series of never-ending choices. Who? What? When? Where? How? It can be very overwhelming at times and extremely challenging to figure things out. How can we be sure that we are making the correct choices?

We don't know what to do, so we seek guidance. We talk to family, friends, peers, co-workers, neighbors, strangers, and we'll even consider consulting the mystics for direction, anyone we think might be able to steer us in the right direction.

Some say, "Talk to God." Now that can seem a bit scary, weird, unbelievable, and unorthodox, as well as an impossible feat to carry out. How can I talk to Him? How can I talk to God?

What if I said that quite possibly you might have already heard the voice of God but just didn't recognize it? Many would say, "Prove it!" Okay, here goes.

The first thing we have to do is to demystify the voice of God. It typically isn't the loud, booming, thunderous vibration that we have imagined. Nor is it an ear-piercing shouting sound that makes the earth quake. Actually, it is quite the opposite. The voice of God sounds like a human voice, in particular, your own voice. In fact, you could have heard the voice of God before, but referred to it as "intuition," a "gut feeling," something that told you what to do, or something that you sensed to do. That which you heard could very easily have been the voice of God.

There is a story of a young boy who was sent to live in a type of monastery with a priest. One night, while the boy was asleep, he was awakened by someone calling his name. "Samuel, Samuel," the voice called out. Samuel got up from his bed and went to the priest to see what he needed. He said to the priest, "Eli, I heard you call, so I came to see you." But Eli answered, "I didn't call you. Go back to bed."

Samuel returned to his bed and fell back asleep. Then, yet again, he was awakened by someone calling his name, "Samuel, Samuel." Again, he went to Eli, the priest, but Eli told Samuel a second time that he had not called for him and that he should return to his bed and rest.

Samuel took a while to fall back to sleep this time, but he did. Then the voice called to him again: "Samuel, Samuel." As before, Samuel went to Eli to see what he needed. This time, Eli had a revelation of who might have been calling Samuel. He told Samuel, "When you hear the voice call you again, say, 'Yes, Lord, I hear you.'"

Maybe, like Samuel, the voice of God has called to us, but we didn't know that it was God. The voice of God might sound like you because He's speaking to you and through you. Feel free to check out a book I wrote on this subject entitled *How To Hear God.*[2]

This is a Thompson Truth!

2. My books are all available on my site:
       www.bentonthompsoniii.com/shop

NOW, WRITE YOUR TRUTH:

_____

_____

_____

_____

_____

_____

_____

_____

_____

_____

_____

_____

_____

_____

_____

_____

8

Time Is Not of the Essence

Many of us have heard and been taught most of our lives that time is of the essence. We've heard things like "Be sure to be on time!" "Don't waste time!" "What time are we supposed to be there?" "What time is it?" Time, time, time! I6t seems that's all you hear.

Mankind has been infatuated with time for a long time (pun intended). Thousands of years ago, devices were invented to measure and keep track of time. The

Egyptians, the Persians, and the ancient Greeks were all obsessed with time But what if I told you that time doesn't really matter? Many would think that I am crazy to say such a thing, that I must have lost my mind. Just hear me out, please.

When we go to God about something, we usually frame our request with certain time constraints. We tell God that we need or want something done by a certain time. "God, when will You do this for me?" "God, I need this done by ____." "God, it has been _____, and it is still not done." All of these are based on time. The problem with that thinking is that God is not time-conscious like we are. God is eternally existent. He is perpetual. In fact, one of the names of God is the Eternal.

This means that where God is time is not relevant nor essential. Simply put, time is not of the essence with God. Allow me to explain this statement a bit further.

Time was created to measure events that occur within a space. How long did it take to get from this point to that point? This is what time tells us. Let's look at what happened in Creation relative to time.

In the beginning, God created by forming from nothing the heavens and the earth. Nothing existed before God, only emptiness. God existed before there were events to measure. In fact, He created the first event. This means that God existed before time. Therefore, He is not dictated to by time.

Notice how God speaks. He uses phrases like *"In the beginning," "in the fullness of time," "for everything there is a season," "everything will be made beautiful in its own time."* God doesn't use a watch, a calendar, or an almanac to answer us. It's all about timing, not time.

Remember, I said that time was created to measure how long it takes to get from one point to the next point. Well, God sees the beginning and the end in the same space with no time lapses. He is the Alpha and the Omega at the same time. He is both the Beginning of all things and the End of everything at the exact same moment. He is All!

God is never in a hurry because He is always on time. He operates beyond the limits of the natural laws that we live

by. God's timing, however, is perfect.
When we learn to completely count on
Him, then it will be God's time.

This is a Thompson Truth!

NOW, WRITE YOUR TRUTH:

_____

_____

_____

_____

_____

_____

_____

_____

_____

_____

_____

_____

_____

_____

_____

_____

_____

9

Thoughts and Prayers

"Thoughts and prayers" is an expression or phrase that is frequently used when someone is ill, hurting, or has suffered loss. Examples are a natural disaster, some other tragedy, or anytime someone is believed to be heavily burdened. It is an offering of condolences or an expression of sorrow. Thoughts and prayers really do play an important role in a person's life during these times.

As I wrote this, I was really hurting inside. I had just recently experienced another loss of a family member. My little brother, Zachary, suddenly passed away in September of 2020. My mind was all over the place. I had thoughts filled with memories of the past, thoughts of his current passing, and thoughts of the unmaterialized future we had planned together for ourselves. My family and I, like so many others, needed the thoughts and prayers of others at this trying time in our life.

Contrary to what some might think, I was not mad at God. In fact, I knew my brother was in his best state ever. The best possible place he could have been was in Heaven with God, but I was hurting because I missed him so much.

When someone truly commits to direct or offer loving thoughts and prayers for you, it is greatly needed and appreciated. Their thoughts can cover your mind from acting out crazy thoughts you might have of your own. You might have them, but a barrier is placed by the kind thoughts of others to keep you from carrying them out. Their prayers will hold your heart and soul in care and comfort.

Some might consider the phrase "thoughts and prayers" an inconsequential act by someone who just doesn't want to get involved, a token show of support, if you will. But nothing could be further from the truth. When one offers their *thoughts and prayers,* it is a way of recognizing that the person really needs God's presence and compassion to help them during this tough time in their life. That's why we should offer our "thoughts and prayers" when anyone we know has a heavy burden to bear.

At times, we might not have prayed as we promised, or we might not have given this person's afflictions a second thought. But now we will, because we know it makes a difference. We need each other's thoughts and prayers, not only in tough times, but at all times.

This is a Heavy and Heartfelt Thompson Truth!

NOW, WRITE YOUR TRUTH:

_____

_____

_____

_____

_____

_____

_____

_____

_____

_____

_____

_____

_____

_____

_____

_____

10

The Religion of Religion
(Part 1)

It is estimated that some 83% of the 7.3 billion global population associate with some form of institutionalized system of religion. By population, Christianity is recorded as the most popular religion, having 31% adherence with 2.3 billion people participating. In the U.S., religion annually contributes more than $1.2 trillion dollars of socioeconomic value to the economy.

What is religion? When did it begin? What is the purpose of it? These are all common questions that get asked every day by people all over the world. I must admit that I, too, am curious as to how this all began.

How did things get so far removed from the beginning concepts? How did the God of Creation and His very personal and individual relationships with people become a cult-like, social-cultural behemoth, an organized system, with designated behaviors and practices? Let's take a look back at how things first began as it relates to Christianity.

The Bible begins with the accounts of one man, Adam, and his relationship with his Creator, God. Adam had a wife and a family, with whom he shared the details about his personal experiences with God.

In the Bible, beginning at the book of Genesis, going all the way through the Old Testament, continuing into the New Testament and leading right up to Jesus, everything is about this one family's experiences with the same God that Adam had a relationship with.

Even the word *testament*, as in Old and New Testament, refers to one's personal statements of belief and their personal testimonies. In other words, the Bible is about one man and the personal relationship he and his descendants had with the God of all Creation. You can see their linage for yourself in Luke 3:23-38. It is sometimes subtitled Family Records, and it lists every family from Jesus back to Adam. Each had his own personal relationship with God.

God is a God of the individual. That's why we were each uniquely created, intentionally different from one another on purpose and for purpose. God wants a one-on-one personal relationship with each of us. That's why He is referred to as "the God of Moses," "the God of Abraham," "the God of Isaac," "the God of Jacob," and "the God of Jesus." He is also the God of Benton and your God too.

So then, what is religion? By contrast, religion is a social and cultural system steeped in rituals and ceremonial acts. Religion was constructed by humans to promote cooperation in social groups and has been presented as a better overall experience for the community. It attempts to keep everyone on the same page.

This was the same mindset that came into play with hunting. Hunting in groups was more effective than hunting alone. Faith, however, is personal. Your faith is your faith, no one else's.

The Bible mentions several times that things happen *"according to your faith."* Just as your relationship with God is not my relationship with God, in every family you will find each child has a different relationship with the parent/s than another child does. Why? Because each child is different.

The family of God is no exception. We were all created differently, to facilitate a different relationship and response. Religion tries to make everyone conform to the same set of beliefs and desires for all to have the same behavior and responses. In so doing, people are dehumanized, being deprived of their unique qualities. Religion tries to make everyone act like they have the same relationship and same expressions of feelings. However, we all respond differently to different situations.

Many feels ostracized by religion because they do not conform to the norms set by other people. Religion is a tradition formed by man. The Gospel of Mark warns us that the traditions of men can make the Word of God ineffective in our lives. God is not a religion or religious! That's what people do, not God. Instead, God desires a personal relationship with each of us.

My prayer is that we all get to know God personally for ourselves. Gathering isn't the issue; it's the man-made requirements of conduct that are the problem. Yes, we can share our experiences with one another, but we should not try to make others comply to our perspectives and behaviors. That should be reserved as a personal decision for each individual, as God designed it.

This is a Thompson Truth!

NOW, WRITE YOUR TRUTH:

_____

_____

_____

_____

_____

_____

_____

_____

_____

_____

_____

_____

_____

_____

_____

_____

_____

_____

~11~

Scrabble Scrapping

I imagine that most of us are pretty familiar with the ever-popular board game called Scrabble, which turned 90 years old in 2021. There are those who love it (like Ex-President Barak Obama, Ex-President Bill Clinton and his wife Hillary, Martha Stewart, and even the Queen of England, the late Elizabeth II).

Some countries have even declared Scrabble to be an official sport, and someone has written a Scrabble song. No kidding! Look it up.

There are also those who hate Scrabble. Like who? Like a lot of people. For them, there is no song and no game. It just depends upon who you talk to. Here's the backstory on the game.

During the Great Depression of the 1930s, an unemployed New York architect by the name of Alfred Butts figured that folks could use a distraction from all the doom and gloom that was going on in the world at the time. (That part sounds a bit familiar, doesn't it?) So, he decided to create a board game that combined both skill and speed.

He drew the board itself and every game tile piece using his architectural equipment. Hence the structured look of everything in Scrabble. For more than a decade, Alfred tried and failed to sell the idea of his new game.

He first called the game, "It," then "Lexiko," short for Lexicon, then "Criss-Cross Words," but all were unsuccessful. No one wanted any part of this game.

Then, in 1948, James Brunot joined as a business partner and changed the name of the game to Scrabble, which means "to scratch or scrape" and "to scrawl," and the rest is history.

Our Thompson Truth today is called Scrabble Scrapping, as in scrapping for the victory. Those who play Scrabble play to win.

Just as Scrabble is a word game, ironically enough, faith is also a word game. When the world used the word *DEPRESSION* with Alfred Butts, he used the "I" in that word and spelled *INVENTION*. When the world spelled the word *QUIT*, Alfred used the "U" to spell the word *UNRELENTING*. These same lessons can be applied to our faith.

The devil used the Word against Jesus, but Jesus certainly knew the Word and gave it right back to the devil.

The devil came to tempt Jesus using the word *ABUSE*, but Jesus, knowing more of the Word, used the "S" and responded by spelling the word *SUBMIT*, as in *SUBMIT TO GOD*.

The devil came a second time to Jesus and tried Him with the word *PRIDE*, but Jesus responded quickly again, using the "P" to spell the words *PRAISE GOD*.

The devil tried a third time using the words *FOLLOW ME*. Jesus had enough of this foolishness and spelled the word *FLEE*, as in *FLEE FROM ME, FOOL*!

You see, sometimes we try to outsmart the devil when we should simply say to him "BYE BYE" or "FLEE!"

We must be quick to respond with the Word of God when we hear things. When the devil comes to us and uses the word *SICK*, we should "bust" his game up, using the words *WE ARE HEALED BY THE STRIPES OF JESUS*! When the devil comes again to us and uses the word *LACK*, we should give him more words: *NO GOOD THING WILL MY FATHER WITHHOLD FROM ME*! When the devil comes to us using the word *DEFEATED*, we should give him back, *LET THE WEAK SAY, "I AM STRONG"*!

Of course, the devil will come to us and say that we aren't playing fair. That's his job as the accuser. We should expect that from him. The devil's words are always negative, but God's Word is always positive.

This is a word world. God made it with His Word, and the devil wants us to accept the world's words. But we are God's, and we shall use God's Word. It's time we start Scrabble Scrapping with the devil. It's time to WORD UP!

This is a Thompson Truth!

NOW, WRITE YOUR TRUTH:

_____

_____

_____

_____

_____

_____

_____

_____

_____

_____

_____

_____

_____

_____

_____

_____

_____

_____

~12~

We're in the Process

If you're anything like me, then you're probably sick and tired of hearing about "the process." "It's in the process. It will happen eventually. Things take time. Trust the process." I'm just so over all of the process speak and waiting on the process. My question is: Why does there even need to be a process? I began to study process and its purpose, and here's what I learned:

One definition of process is "a sequence of interdependent and linked tasks,

97

that when put together transforms numerous inputs into a specific given output." At each stage in the process, there are various resources, such as people, time, energy, machines, money or whatever else that can be used as inputs to be converted into a particular desired output. These outputs then serve as inputs for the next stage in the process ... until a known goal or end result is reached.

All of that being said, a process is "a series of events which produce a result." The contention is that when a process is used, the goal/assignment is completed at a rate of five times faster than when there is no process in place. Here's an example:

One day Henry Ford took the head of his production team, Charles Sorensen, to an empty building in Detroit, which would eventually become the home of The Ford Motor Company, America's first mass-produced car factory. Ford explained his idea to his manager for a new production process. Instead of using one craftsman to create a singular product by himself, each and every craftsman would be taught to do one of the eighty-four simple, repetitive jobs required to complete the full assembly. With this process in place, the manufacturing time of the Model T Ford was cut significantly from 12.5 hours to 2.5 hours for completion of a single vehicle. This new process built

15 million cars, and amazing success was achieved.

God also has a process for us. And, surprise, WE'RE IN THE PROCESS!

Here's a look at a process God used in the life of a woman named Ruth. She was a young bride whose husband had been suddenly killed. Her mother-in-law lost not only Ruth's husband, but her other son as well. In addition to losing her two sons, she had also recently lost her husband. Both women were utterly mired in tragedy and grief.

The mother-in-law was mortified and decided to return to her homeland. Ruth begged to be allowed to go with her. After much protest, her mother-in-law relented. So the two traveled back to the mother-in-law's homeland where they lived for a time in extreme poverty.

Ruth eventually got a job as a migrant field worker picking up the leftover scraps. She worked hard and diligently every day. One day she was noticed by the wealthy landowner, whom she ultimately fell in love with and married.

God's process changed Ruth's destiny forever and that of her family as well. It involved a lot of time, tears, soul-searching, and people.

Sometimes God's process is on a much shorter cycle. After all, He is in eternity, where He is not bound by time. There have been many accounts given, when someone's process was said to be "instantaneous."

We don't know whether our process is like Henry Ford's, which took more than nineteen years to produce the desired results, like the one used for Ruth, which happened over a twelve-year period, or if it will be instant, as has been the case with others.

However it happens and whenever it happens, the purpose for the process is to get us to our desired destination five times faster. We need to remember this when we are tempted to complain about the process. Were it not for the process, things would take a whole lot longer to come to fruition.

Thank You, Lord, for my process!

This is a hard Thompson Truth!

NOW, WRITE YOUR TRUTH:

_____

_____

_____

_____

_____

_____

_____

_____

_____

_____

_____

_____

_____

_____

_____

_____

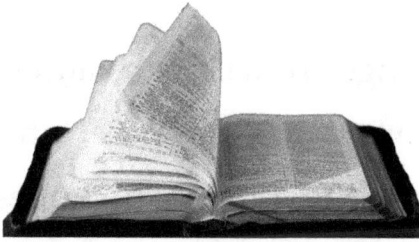

~13~

We Can't Lose Hope

No matter what, we can't lose hope! It will be okay if we lose our way. Hope will help us find it again. It will be okay if we lose our income. Hope will help us get more. It will be okay even if we lose a loved one. Hope will get us through it. I say this from my own personal experiences with losing my little brother and previously having lost my mother and two sisters over a few years.

If, however, we lose hope, then we will have lost all possibility of expecting any future change in our circumstances. To have hope means to have an expectation. Take, for example, a woman who hopes to bear a child. She must first be expecting before there can be any possibility of her dream coming true. Hope will impregnate you with expectation, and it takes expectation to deliver your desires. If you are not expecting, there will be no delivery!

Each of us will face tough times in our life, no matter who we are or where we live. No matter how strong, how powerful, or how confident we believe we are, tough times will still come our way and pressure us to give up, cave in, and crumble.

Fear of the unknown tries to bully and rob you of any hopes of expecting a future change of circumstances that you might have. The toughest challenge we will face during any situation in our life is to not lose hope!

Perhaps you feel trapped under the rocks of your situation, you're not sleeping at night, and you can't see your way free from this thing that grips you. It feels like all hope is lost. Still, we cannot lose hope. Hope means everything to us.

Hope is much more than an optimistic state of mind that is based on an expectation of positive outcomes with respect to the events in your life. Hope is more than feeling good about things. Hope is not wishing for something magical to happen. Hope is an essential piece in the foundation toward seeing what you desire to have happen. Hope is the hinge on the doors of opportunity that will open us up to new and creative possibilities.

A long time ago there were a great number of people who were taken captive during a terrible war. The people were kept in captivity for several years. They prayed and prayed, yet saw no change. Hope was all but lost. One day a believer was sent to give them this word of Hope: *"I know what I am doing. I have it all planned out—plans to take care of you, not to abandon you, plans to give you the future you've been hoping for."* No matter how long it has been, nor how bad it has gotten, God still has a plan for us, and the plan is to give us the future we have been hoping for. That is very encouraging to me, and I hope it is to you too. No matter how bad things look or how bad we feel, we must still have the audacity to hope.

Hope is the only hope we have. So, let us hold unswervingly to the hope we profess, for He who promised is faithful!

This is a Thompson Truth!

NOW, WRITE YOUR TRUTH:

_____

_____

_____

_____

_____

_____

_____

_____

_____

_____

_____

_____

_____

_____

_____

_____

14

How Do You Follow God?

I imagine that we've all probably heard, at one time or another, someone speak about following God. Some say they have been following Him for years, while others might say they have only recently begun following Him. Which begs the question: How do you follow God? Where is He? And where is He going? Is there some sort of a map involved? Has a personal guide been provided to show us the way? Will there be signs indicating how far we have to travel to reach the desired destination?

Seekers like you and me have so many questions. One of the first questions that needs an answer is: Why should I follow God? To answer this, let's try applying the same logic for why we would want to follow any other person.

One of the reasons we might want to follow someone is that we are lost. If you find yourself in uncharted and unfamiliar territory and you don't know where you are going, it might make sense to follow someone who does.

Another situation might be when you don't know what to do, which way to turn? Many of us might consider asking guidance from someone we think could help us. Or it might be that you are just tired, you've been exhausted by the journey of never-ending roadblocks, detours, and rerouting because of something you didn't know about, and now you're willing to follow someone, anyone, who could lead you to your destination.

Okay, and why follow God? He created us, and no one knows us better than He does. If we're going to trust anyone to offer guidance or direction to us, then God would certainly qualify as a great choice.

We have a direct quote from Him on this: *"I will guide you along the best pathway for your life. I will advise you and watch over you."* That sounds very convincing, but let's put it to the test.

"God, I don't know the way to happiness. Which way should I go?" "God, I'm not sure which choice to make. Will You help me?" "God, I'm struggling with some things and I don't know where to turn." It has been said many times that men refuse to ask for directions. If you don't ask for directions, you will never get directions.

If you have ever followed someone, you know how important it is to stick close. To follow God, we must surely stick very close, close to what He says, and close to what He does.

When we decide to follow God, it means that He goes first. The only way we can follow Him is if He's in front of us. He's first! We're not leading; He is.

Following is not about being in agreement with the leader; it's about submitting to their guidance and direction. Why? Because we have made a decision to trust them.

Another tip for following someone is to not to allow anything to come between you and the person you're following. Don't allow anything to block your view of that person. And following God is no different.

Some might wonder, "How can anything block the view of God? God is huge! Isn't God too big for anything to block the view of Him?" The sun is one hundred times larger than planet Earth, and yet you can block the view of it with your hand. This proves it doesn't take something very big to block your view of God.

Let's say that we agree to follow God. Where do we begin? To give us an idea of where to begin, I looked into how a private detective would follow someone, and this is what I found: First, the detective will study the person they are to follow, researching them to try to get to know them and their tendencies. Next, they memorize the features of who they are following as to recognize them in different situations and settings. This will keep them from being fooled when things look different than they expect.

Next, as we noted earlier, when following someone, always make sure to keep them in your sight, not allowing anything to block your view, while still maintaining a fair distance of separation. The detective is not trying to predict what will happen; he is just observing the reality of what's happening.

Lastly, I found, a good detective or good follower is always alert and attentive to who they are following. *To follow* means "to go after or go behind someone in the same direction they are going." Get more insights from my book, *How to Follow God.*[3]

This is a Thompson Truth!

3. My books are all available on my site:
www.bentonthompsoniii.com/shop

NOW, WRITE YOUR TRUTH:

_____

_____

_____

_____

_____

_____

_____

_____

_____

_____

_____

_____

_____

_____

_____

_____

_____

_____

15

Have I Sinned?

Sin ... Have I sinned? If so, when did I sin? And how did I sin? These are all legitimate questions one might ask, especially someone who is focused on gaining more insight into God and perhaps even considering a closer relationship with Him.

We have been told that sin is the cornerstone issue that exists between man and God and that we cannot have a close relationship with Him because of it. But I personally haven't yet heard anyone give a simplistic and easily comprehensible understanding of what sin is. In order to honestly answer whether or not I have sinned, I must have a full understanding of what sin is. Here is my attempt to share with you what sin is. I received an understanding of SIN, through an acronym:

The "S" is for *Separation.*

Sin usually takes place when we are away from others, those whom we trust for good advice, when we are isolated, either in actuality or in our thoughts. We are separated from family, friends, or other trusted sources.

The "I" is for *Information*.

During our time of separation and isolation, we receive some information. Something is presented to us that we had not previously considered, or if we did, we declined it before. Now it has come back to us again to reconsider. It is tempting and taunting, inviting us to give something we would not normally considered a try. We sense this information is a bit sketchy, but we are considering it nonetheless.

The "N" is for *Noncompliance*.

When we are separated and receive some sketchy information, we are then given a choice, a choice to either continue to comply with what had previously been our standard of truth and rightness or to succumb to the change and go with this new and somewhat sketchy idea that has come to us.

Let's say we decide to choose noncompliance. When we make that decision to be noncompliant, to no longer hold fast to the truths we know have been foundational for us, simply put, *this* is when we sin.

Here is a statement of truth that I believe best explains sin: *"If anyone, then, knows the good they ought to do and doesn't do it, it is sin for them."* Sin is not an act, but rather a defiant mindset that causes you to act in a particular manner that you previously deemed wrong or incorrect.

A good example would be the first sin on record. A young man was contemplating killing his brother because he had given a better gift, and he was jealous. Hear what he was told: *"If you desire to do what is right, will you not be accepted? But if you do not what is right, sin is crouching at your door; it desires to have you, but you must rule over it."*

S.I.N.—During separation, in comes counter information, and then we choose noncompliance and override previously-held standards of known truth. So now back to the original question: Have I sinned? My answer is: Yes, every time I exercise my free will to do what I know is not the right thing to do, I have sinned.

But hope is not lost. God sent His Son to be the propitiation or substitute for our collective sins, and we can still get back close to Him. Thank God! So, with that, we must go and sin no more.

This is a Thompson Truth!

NOW, WRITE YOUR TRUTH:

_____

_____

_____

_____

_____

_____

_____

_____

_____

_____

_____

_____

_____

_____

_____

_____

_____

16

Worryful

Do not be concerned because you have never heard of this word before. *Worryful* is a word that I came up with to describe a person who believes in the power of worrying.

Everyone worries. We all do it. Worrying is when you feel uneasy or troubled by something that could happen. No matter where we are in our faith, whether beginners or veterans, we still worry. But does it help? Let us examine the power of worrying and how it affects our situations.

Worrying makes us feel like we are doing something. It keeps us from feeling helpless. Worrying occupies our thoughts, and we hope it will prevent us from experiencing the worst outcome.

Did you know that worrying has the power to make you sick? Yes, hence the saying, "I've been worried sick about that." Worrying can make you short tempered, because you haven't gotten the proper rest and nutrition. Worrying can cause tension, poor sleep, irritability, fatigue, problems concentrating, and general unhappiness. In other words, when weu worry, we torment ourselves.

If worrying has so many drawbacks, then why do we do it? We believe it is a way of showing that we care or are concerned. We tell ourselves that worrying might help us solve the problem.

Sometimes we worry simply because we don't know what else to do. But worrying draws negative thoughts and energy to us. Worry breeds thoughts, images, emotions, and actions of negativity that continue to repeat over and over again in many variations of a possible bad outcome.

We sometimes feel that if we can imagine the worst, then perhaps we can prevent it from happening. This process produces anxiety rather than a solution. Worry is anxiousness. We try to anticipate what we believe could happen. The problem is that worry anticipates negativity. It assumes the outcome will not be favorable.

If worrying predicted favorable outcomes, then we would be celebrating, and I, for one, have never celebrated the things I worried about. What, then, should we do? God says that we should cast all our anxieties/cares on Him because He cares for us. How can we do that? Let me tell you what I do.

I try to live in the present moment. This can be challenging, but I still try to remain in the present, not the past, and not the future. As for the things I am concerned about in the possible future, I write them down. I list them all out, one by one. Then I get a huge envelope to put them in. I write "GOD" on the outside of the envelope and put it away in my closet. That is His now. In this way, I cast my cares on the One who cares for me.

This is not me being irresponsible, but rather me trusting God to care about my cares. After all, these are future potential problems that have not yet happened and might never happen.

For more helpful tips on trusting God, see my book *How to Trust God*.[4]

This is a Thompson Truth!

---

4. My books are all available on my site:
      www.bentonthompsoniii.com/shop

NOW, WRITE YOUR TRUTH:

_____

_____

_____

_____

_____

_____

_____

_____

_____

_____

_____

_____

_____

_____

_____

_____

_____

_____

17

Timing Tells Time

Many times, we are focused solely on time. Society at large puts great emphasis on time. "What time is it?" "What time do we have to be there?" "What time is he coming?" "What time should we launch the new project (new CD, new clothing line, etc.)?" Time... Time... Time! Even though we are so consumed with time, however, we don't seem to give a lot of consideration to timing. Do we assume that time will tell timing when things are ready? Is time really all that much more important than timing?

No, nothing could be further from the truth. Timing is everything. Timing tells time when things are ready, not the other way around. Timing is a supernatural function, while time is a natural function. Which is to say, time is man-made. Take a clock, for example. On the other hand, timing cannot be dictated nor constructed by man.

Time usually deals with the occurrence of one single event, whereas timing has to do with the alignment of the occurrence of several events. We are typically concerned with one problem, one issue, one challenge. God's resolution to our one thing might require the collaboration of several things.

For example, you might be having a problem at work with a supervisor. God's solution could require that He touch the hearts and lives of several people who could help influence a change of heart in your supervisor. This could take several days. The problem comes when we are expecting our one small thing to be resolved instantly.

When we pray, God hears and grants that request immediately—providing, of course, that it is in line with His character and nature. However, the fulfillment of that request might require a process, and that process requires timing.

So, the go forward lesson is this: When the timing is right (meaning all things needed for the fulfillment are properly aligned and in place), we will receive the answer to our prayer. Always remember, timing tells time.

This is a Thompson Truth!

NOW, WRITE YOUR TRUTH:

_____

_____

_____

_____

_____

_____

_____

_____

_____

_____

_____

_____

_____

_____

_____

_____

_____

18

Itty Bitty Faith

I'm guessing that when many of you saw this title, you probably said to yourself, "Where in the world is he going with this?" Well, let me tell you.

When it comes to having faith, or as I often say "faithing" for something, many of us might be a bit apprehensive at times. The apprehension comes in the form of the question: Do I have enough faith to believe for what I am believing for? Sometimes just the very thought alone of asking for something can be a nerve-wracking experience by itself. That is before we also consider the fact that we must stand, wait, and act like we believe it will happen, in order to get it to happen. Sheesh!

That can be a tall order for any of us, but there is hope. We might think an undertaking like this would require great faith. But, no, it doesn't, not even a good amount of faith. It only requires itty bitty faith! Let me show you.

Teeny Tiny ... Itsy Bitsy ... Itty Bitty ... These phrases all indicate the same thing, "a very small amount or portion size." That's all the faith that is required by God to see your prayers answered.

I know that to our natural minds that doesn't make sense. We normally think you must bet big to win big. But with God things work a bit differently.

In my faith manual, I focused on two separate references to the amount of faith we should have. In the first reference, we are told to observe the tiniest of all creatures—an ant. An ant could be easily stepped on by any of us, blown away by a good breeze, washed away by a light rain, or disposed of very easily by something that we would consider insignificant. Yet, the ant endures, unfazed by any of it.

It is reported that an ant can lift ten times its own weight, objects much bigger than itself. How is that even possible? It is because of the faith that ant has.

Which brings me to the second reference on faith that I saw in the faith manual. It says that we only need to have faith the size of a mustard seed. To gain perspective, I went to a grocery store and purchased some mustard seeds. They are really quite small, one might even say, itty bitty. In the palm of an average adult hand, one could easily hold more than two hundred mustard seeds. I know this because I tried it with my own hand. And all we need is the amount of faith the size of one of these seeds—just one of them!

An ant is slightly larger than a mustard seed, yet it has mustard-seed faith. I wonder what we could lift, carry, or endure if we exercised some itty bitty faith.

I've provided myself with constant reminders of the amount of faith I need to have for the things that I am "faithing" for all around me. I placed a mustard seed beside several light switches and doorways in my home, in my vehicle, at work, and I carry one in my pocket. So, wherever I go, wherever I am, I remind myself I only need the itty bitty faith of the mustard seed to go on.

Our faith will grow just like the mustard seed when we bury it down deep on the inside of us, where it can take root and be fed by the watering of our words. Words like "I can," "I will," and "I believe" will all water our itty bitty, mustard-seed faith!

This is a Thompson Truth!

NOW, WRITE YOUR TRUTH:

_____

_____

_____

_____

_____

_____

_____

_____

_____

_____

_____

_____

_____

_____

_____

~19~

Believing for Dummies

A lot of people might think that believing is difficult, but I have found a way to simplify it. Believing does not come as easy for those who think they are of high intelligence, those who think their intelligence can figure anything out. Believing works better for those of us who concede that we don't know everything, nor can we.

Believing means you just came to a place of trust, trusting in the unseen and the unknown, a place where we can say, "I don't have to understand a thing to believe it."

A passage in my faith manual says this, *"Eyes have not seen, ears have not heard, neither has any person even considered just how much God loves them as an individual."* In other words, we cannot even fathom just how much God loves us. We're just going to have to believe it.

Faith is like hoping so, while believing is like knowing so. How can we go from hoping to believing? Well, I'm glad you asked.

We should do it the same way we grew in faith. When we began in faith, we began small. We took a little something that we could "faith" for. Or perhaps we had several small things we were "faithing" for. Either way, the principle was the same. Then, one day, somehow, something happened that we were "faithing" for. We got down on our knees and thanked God that it finally happened. (Hopefully, we all did that. If not, we still have time to do it.) Then we moved on to something else that we were "faithing" for, and eventually it, too, came to pass.

At different times, we received something we had "faithed" for. Our faith was growing. Over time, which can vary by person and situation, we had several things come to pass that we had been "faithing" for.

Before you say, "Not me," just take a moment to reflect. Look back over your life, and I am sure you will see something that you "faithed" for once that came to pass. Hopefully, we all can find something that happened which we were "faithing" for.

I have a huge manila envelope that contains things I am "faithing" for. I call it my Faith Safe. In there, I have locked away all the things I am "faithing" for. Those things are between me and God only.

As time progressed and things changed, I created another new manila folder. This new folder became my "I Believe Briefcase." Contained in it are the things I know God has done for me. These things were not coincidences, good luck, or good fortune. These are things I know personally that God did. I know this because no one knew but God some of the things I was "faithing" for. Whether they were too big, or too personal, no one knew but me and God, and I locked them away in my Faith Safe.

As some of these have materialized in God's perfect timing, I moved them over to the I Believe Briefcase. Just as my Faith Safe has grown, so too will my I Believe Briefcase, one small personal thing at a time.

In the past, I have asked a question, and someone has answered, "I believe so." That "I believe so" meant, "I hope so" or "I think so." God wants our "I believe so" to mean that we "know so" because we have experienced it to be so.

There have been things I experienced that I can say "I believe so." I believe that God is merciful. I know this because there have been many, many times when I was in the wrong, and yet He spared me. As a result, I believe and know that God is merciful.

Here is another example: I believe that God is gracious. I believe this because I do not get what I deserve. I deserve hurt for the hurt I have caused, but I believe God is gracious. He doesn't give me what I deserve; He gives me His unconditional love instead.

Some might be wondering why I have a Faith Safe and a Believing Briefcase. The Faith Safe locks away all my private and personal requests, while my Believing

Briefcase is to be shared with others, so that I can help their faith to grow too.

If you have not already begun your Faith Safe, I encourage you to start one right now. For those who already have a Faith Safe, consider starting your Believing Briefcase so that you can share your testimonies with others, to help them start their Faith Safe.

Some of the toughest times I've had believing were when I failed to review the contents of my Faith Safe. My process is so simple. That is why I call it Believing for Dummies, dummies like me.

This is a Thompson Truth!

NOW, WRITE YOUR TRUTH:

_____

_____

_____

_____

_____

_____

_____

_____

_____

_____

_____

_____

_____

_____

_____

_____

_____

20

A Fight To Obey

What first comes to mind when you hear the word *obey*? Do you cringe? Are you indifferent or does some form of defiance rise up in you? Maybe, like many, you believe obedience is archaic, outdated, and has no place in today's society. Perhaps an image flashes in your mind of an instance when someone was attempting to control you, and so they required you to obey them.

We all have different reactions to the use of the word *obey*. That is because of our own personal predisposition to what we believe obey means. Some women feel repulsed at the sound of the word, believing it to mean they are to become a mindless slave to a cruel master. Similarly, there are men who hate hearing the word *obey* in reference to them. Why? Because they feel it involves their emasculation. Even the youth get involved with the rejection of the word *obey*, because they feel it stifles their freedom of expression. In very many cases, whatever the reason, you can easily find a fight to obey.

I am reminded of an anecdote my father shared with me and my eight siblings. If you see everyone is going in the same direction and you decide to join them, make sure you know who you're joining.

There is a huge difference between a mob and a movement. This got me to wondering: Why is there such a great resistance to obeying?

As I explored my manual on faith, I found that God mentions *"obey"* several times throughout it. Is it possible that there is a connection between faith and obedience?

As I continued reading and studying, I found that even Jesus had an issue with obeying. It says that it was important that He learned to obey. Hmm! Even Jesus had to learn how to obey. Wow!

This was confirmation to me that there must be a connection between faith and obeying. So, as I studied further and received a greater understanding, this is what I got:

As we grow in our faith, we will eventually become believers. Things we previously accepted by faith, we learn to be the truth, and we are now believers of the truth.

Faith is simply a trust in the unseen. We grow and walk in faith, on the legs of obeying the truth that we hear. And the more we obey, the stronger our faith grows.

As we continue obeying (and thus continue growing), we will see the things that we trusted in being manifested right before our very eyes. That is why the fight to obey is so vicious. Obedience serves as a key to unlock the manifestation to what we have been "faithing" for.

This is a Thompson Truth!

NOW, WRITE YOUR TRUTH:

_____

_____

_____

_____

_____

_____

_____

_____

_____

_____

_____

_____

_____

_____

_____

_____

21

Imaginary Faith
(Part 1)

When most of us hear the word *imaginary*, we might think of something that's not real. It's fake, just something that's made up, pretend, like the Easter Bunny or Santa Claus. Faith could be thought of in this same way. It is a hope that something will happen, and then a pretending that it already has.

But isn't pretending a bad thing? We all did it as children, but we're adults now.

We can't just sit around all day imagining "stuff," like we're Peter Pan. Besides, isn't imagination something that is used heavily in the occult? Yes, it is.

But also consider this: drug dealers, drug users, housewives, single parents, children, murderers, the elderly, and hardworking people all ride in cars. What's the point? Imagination is just a vehicle that can transport you between realities.

Faith is transcendent and reaches its highest potential when you add in imagination. God uses imagination, and He wholeheartedly believes in the power of it.

A long time ago, there was a group of refugees who settled in a desert plains area. They wanted to build a mighty fortified city the size of Chicago, complete with walls and a huge tower. They wanted their tower to be seen from all around the region, even from outer space. They imagined building a tower as high as the heavens.

When God saw this strange activity, this was His response: *"And the LORD said, 'Behold, the people is one, and they have all one language; and this they begin to do: and now nothing will be restrained from them, which they have imagined to do'"* (Genesis 11:6). This is one example or proof that God believes in the power of imagination.

The area where those refugees settled was called Babylon, which is now current-day Iraq, and science has once again confirmed the Bible by using archaeological evidence. Reports show that the building of the tower was attempted twice, once with the early citizens of Shinar (Babylon), and then again with one of its kings (Nebuchadnezzar II).

Nebuchadnezzar attempted rebuilding a ziggurat (a rectangular steeped tower) just south of Bagdad. Those ruins have been confirmed and are believed to be from the biblical Tower of Babylon.

The atomic bomb, the first flight, the polio vaccine, the electric light, the death ray, and cellphones all came to light because of someone's imagination. God created the entire world and all the universes out of His imagination. We must ask ourselves: What are we building from our imagination? Is it good? Is it helpful? Is it what we want for ourselves?

Our minds can be a formidable opponent or a great asset on the path to having a better life. The imagination plays a big role in that. When things are not going well, it can dredge up all kinds of negative images, to derail you with doubt and fear ... if you let it. Developing a good and healthy imagination is one of the great challenges of life.

Your mind aims your life on the trajectory path it will follow. It dictates your perception and reception. Unlike other things that you can claim mastery over after a finite amount of time, the mind can sometimes take a lifetime to master. The challenge is putting in the work every single day.

Everyone was once a child, and there are things you experienced that were outside of your control. Regardless of their severity, those experiences stayed with you, and those experiences became part of your story. Overcoming the story you tell yourself about your own experience can be quite a life challenge.

Whether you grew up poor, didn't have a lot of love in your home, or didn't feel seen, it affects the way you move through the world. There are the facts of these experiences, and then there are fuzzy edges where our minds fill in the blanks.

For example: if you say, "I grew up poor and I am always going to be poor," that is an example of your story taking control. Comparatively, if you say, "I grew up poor, but I'm working hard now, doing whatever I can to make sure I have all the things I need and am comfortable," even if it's hard, that is still an example of overcoming your story.

I grew up in and out of apartments, worried about money, with feelings of unworthiness because of what I saw around me. I thought struggling was normal and survival was a default mode of being. And it all became part of my story. As an adult, however, I had to make a choice. Either I would allow past experiences to shape my current narrative or I could focus on the circumstances of the present as a reflection of my current reality.

While the choice may be clear, the action required to shift the narrative is challenging. It requires intentionality and self-awareness. You have to be willing to let go of the stories that don't serve you anymore, in favor of exploring the present moment to the fullest. Carrying around stale, negative narratives stifles your ability to engage in positive self-reflection, which is the cornerstone of personal growth.

When you have set your story aside in favor of embracing the present, you encourage others to do the same. Overcoming your story empowers you to embrace the moment as an opportunity to write a new story, one you are in control of. On the road to becoming a better person, focusing on what you can control and letting go of what you can't control is critical.

This is a Thompson Truth!

NOW, WRITE YOUR TRUTH:

_____

_____

_____

_____

_____

_____

_____

_____

_____

_____

_____

_____

_____

_____

_____

22

The Religion of Religion
(Part 2)

Religion has become a huge part of the human experience. Almost everyone practices some form of institutionalized religion. A world report done in 2020 showed that more than twenty religions are adhered worldwide. The top five religions that are practiced, based on population, are Christianity, Buddhism, Hinduism, Islam, and Other.

Here they are in ranking order: #1 Christianity–31%, #2 Islam–24%. Most of us are not surprised that these two are the most prevalent ones. However, many will likely be surprised by #3. Can you guess which it is? Here's a hint. Its not Buddhism or Hinduism. Wow! Who knew? Yes, it's Other.

The #3 world religion is Other, also called non-religious, irreligious, or unaffiliated, having 15% with 1.2 billion people in adherence. We are seeing a growing number of people who do not want to be associated with any organized religion.

Which brings us to this point: many people want to intertwine religion with faith, as though they were interchangeable, and they're not. Religion is something that was crafted by humans, as a coalition or organization that would be separate from secular society, for people who worshiped their god, whatever their god. Having faith and belief in the same god are what make up a community of worshippers in that god.

Some religions have several gods they worship, while others worship only one god. Still, faith should never automatically be linked to religion. Religion or religious, at its core, just means repetitiveness. For example, "Jimmy religiously washes his car every Saturday morning." Notice, there's no mention of worshipping God referenced here. It is just a repetitive act.

Faith, on the other hand, involves a relationship, which speaks of loyalty, trust, fidelity, and commitment to one held in a high regard. It takes courage to have faith in the Living God of Abraham, Isaac, Jacob, Jesus, you, and me, courage to be willing to step away from the safety of conventional knowledge and the usual way of gathering information, courage to step into an unknown, unseen, not concise, realm of shadows, mysteries, and ancient writings and trust it with everything in you, courage to declare that I believe that the Creator of the Universe is God, my heavenly Father.

The very definition of faith is described as *"the substance of things hoped for and the evidence of the unseen."* Many ascribe to the notion that by using this definition of faith, one can hope or believe for anything, and it will happen. That would be hocus pocus, not faith. The definition of faith is not referring to one's personal, and self-serving ambitions. It refers to having conviction to stand and believe in the unseen things that God has promised to us in His Word.

Although I cannot see it now, yet I believe it to be so, because You have said it, Lord. That is faith, believing without having to see it first.

Faith is irrational to the natural mindset, but so, too, was flying or a driverless car. Faith cannot be rationalized; it must be realized.

Religion can be very restrictive in terms of expression and conduct. Religion preaches unwavering uniformity, which is impossible for uniquely created individuals. Religion requires repetitiveness: "Wear this," "Pray this," "Say that," "Do this," etc., etc., etc. God says only, *"Come unto me all who are tired [tired of], and I will give you rest."*

Interestingly enough, religion or religious is never mentioned once in the Old Testament, and only in three places in the New Testament, all of them having a negative connotation.

Here is a message that Jesus offered to those who were religious in His day: *"Woe to you, teachers of the law and Pharisees, you hypocrites! You travel over land and seas to win a single convert, and once you have succeeded, you make them twice as much a child of hell as you are."* Those who love and worship God will do so in spirit and in truth, not in an organization.

Too often we are eager to go and gather in a building or in a meeting in front of others, to profess our love and commitment for God before we have first gathered in our heart before God and shared that affirmation with Him privately.

Religious people killed Jesus because He did not subscribe to their code of conduct. I have no desire to be religious with God, but I do desire to be faithful to Him.

This is a Thompson Truth!

NOW, WRITE YOUR TRUTH:

_____

_____

_____

_____

_____

_____

_____

_____

_____

_____

_____

_____

_____

_____

_____

_____

_____

_____

IMAGINARY FAITH
(Part 2)

Is imaginary faith really something we should be exploring? It has to be sacrilegious or something, doesn't it? I've never heard of such a thing before. What does God have to say about all this? I'm glad you asked.

"Now to him who is able to do immeasurably more than all we can ask or imagine, according to his power that is at work within us" (Ephesians 3:20).

Wow! Who knew that God wants to do immeasurably more for us than we could even imagine?

Yes, He does, but there is just one catch. We must be able to imagine what we have asked for. Yes, you must see it first with the eyes of your spirit, or you will never actually see it.

We have all asked and asked and asked some more. Right? The problem was not with the asking; the problem was with imagining being done that which we asked for. This means that all this time we've been holding ourselves back due to our lack of imagination. It wasn't that man, it wasn't that woman, and it wasn't the devil. It wasn't even God. It was us!

The Word of God tells us that we were made in the very image of God, and *image* is the root word of *imagination*. This means we were created by God's imagination or His imaginary faith. God imagined you and me long before He made us.

The proof is in the pudding, as they say. Well, let's have some pudding then. *"Before I began to form you in the womb, I knew you, and before you came out of the womb to be born, I set selected you, and set you apart from others; I called and appointed you to be my prophet to the nations"*(Jeremiah 1:5).

God told Jeremiah, *"I saw you before I saw you,"* and the same can be said for each of us. God saw us before He saw us.

Now that's pretty powerful when you think about it. God saw/imagined you and me being better and doing better than we are right now. God saw/imagined us happier than we are right now! God saw/imagined us more peaceful than we are right now. God saw/imagined us healthier than we are right now. God saw/ imagined us wealthier than we are right now!

Notice I didn't say richer, because riches are limited, but wealth is generational. Riches just means you've got "stuff"; wealth shows you have the wisdom to know what to do with the "stuff" once you get it.

According to the New York Daily News, some 70% of lottery winners (riches) end up completely broke within seven years of receiving the money. Even worse, the report goes on to show that several winners have died untimely and horrible deaths after winning, and many have witnessed those closest to them die, without even being able to help them financially. That's why God wants us wealthier, not just richer.

Imagination can be either good or evil. God speaks of those who used *"evil imaginations"* several times throughout His Holy Word. Their end was unpleasant. That's why we're talking about imaginary faith, not just imagination.

Our English word *imagine* is translated from the Greek word *meletao*, which means "to mediate on." So, whenever you see someone in the Bible talking about meditating, they are basically talking about using their imagination.

Joshua, the great warrior and leader, said he was going to meditate/imagine God's Word coming to pass in his life day and night. His imagination gave him numerous victories despite the odds against him.

Abraham mediated/imagined what God could do for him by looking up into the night sky and seeing all the stars. His imagination grew larger after he saw the vast Universe, and he believed that surely God could bless him with one tiny baby, despite the fact that he was nearly a hundred years old.

David, Esther, Ruth, Samson, and Jabez all used their imaginary faith to get results.

Jesus would often go away and meditate/imagine how God could save His life even after others would tragically take it. He saw/imagined His resurrection long before He ever physically saw His resurrection.

How many times have we said, "I can't imagine myself doing _____. I can't imagine myself being _____." Maybe that's been our problem. God is waiting for us to put our imaginary faith to good use. Once we do, He will immensely exceed all our imaginations. Are you ready? Let's get busy using our imaginary faith.

This is a Thompson Truth!

NOW, WRITE YOUR TRUTH:

_____

_____

_____

_____

_____

_____

_____

_____

_____

_____

_____

_____

_____

_____

_____

_____

_____

The Religion of Religion
(Part 3)

This is our third chat on religion. In conclusion, it's worth noting that the ideology of religion itself is not bad, no more than a vehicle which is to be used for the express purpose of transporting people from one destination to the next is bad. A problem occurs in both scenarios when someone perverts the purpose and uses it to imprison, control, dictate, and discriminate against those whom it was supposed to help.

The idea of creating a designated time and space in life, separate from work, to commune with God and address the other needed areas of life is a great idea. However, the word for religion in Latin is *religare*, which means "to bind." Religion, as currently constructed, seeks to bind men, women, and children. The Word of God does not bind us. In fact, God wants us free—*free indeed*!

Religion tends to make people think they can earn their way into Heaven with good deeds. Religion can make people think that God is petty and sits around all day watching, just waiting for an opportunity to unleash His wrath and drop a thunderbolt on those who misbehave.

A plane crash killed a sinner onboard, and the others were just collateral damage because God knew they were going to mess up eventually. The same could be said for that shooting, the flood, the fire, the pandemic, or any other catastrophe that we choose to fault God for.

Religion says a person died because God needed another angel in Heaven. What? The billion or so that He already has wasn't enough? I don't think so!

Religion can make people feel inadequate if they fail to comply with the standards set by a committee, board, or leader.

Religion teaches that when praying you should be a pious performer and impress the people, rather than having a simple chat with God as you would a good friend.

Religion encourages mindless repetition for the good of uniformity and social classism, suggesting that your value or worth is based on your title: Bishop, Archbishop, Evangelist, Pastor, Assistant Pastor, Deacon, Director, Praise Team Leader, Administrator, Member of _____, etc., etc., etc. God addresses us all simply as His children.

To shun being religious, there are those who say they are spiritual. Religion is ritualistic repetitiveness; spiritual just means you're still searching.

Confucius, a notedly spiritual person, had this to say, "If you don't know how to live as a person, how can you serve the spirit?" Being spiritual is but another journey that many go on while trying to decide. The Bible offers these instructions, *"I wish you were hot or cold, not lukewarm."* It is our right and responsibility to make a decision.

This means we can no longer blame the church, a religious group/denomination, a pastor, a church member, a leader, or anyone else, for why we don't have a personal relationship with God.

Religion is a business; faith in God is an intimate personal relationship. Which will you choose?

This is a Thompson Truth!

NOW, WRITE YOUR TRUTH:

_____

_____

_____

_____

_____

_____

_____

_____

_____

_____

_____

_____

_____

_____

_____

24

Cardiosalvation

This message is not about the saving of our hearts, but rather about how our hearts can save us. The Hebrew word for heart is *lêb*, which means "the center of feelings, the will, and the intellect." In other words, our heart is the very center of who we are, our essence, our totality, not what we show, but who we are, our true self.

Our heart is the key to our salvation. Hence the title Cardiosalvation. Salvation means we are the recipients of the grace of God's plan to protect and provide for us as we operate according to His Kingdom principles. Therefore, we shall be saved from the random, spiritless, prejudices and injustices of the world.

As we continue to operate in and apply Kingdom principles to our lives, we shall be saved. But the key to operating in the principles of the Kingdom of God is our heart. The enemy wants our hearts, not our minds. Look at what this parable has to say:

As the principles of the Kingdom are taught/sown among "the people who have heard; then comes the evil one to take the message away from their hearts, so that they will not believe and be saved." This clearly shows that we believe in our hearts, which is the key to our salvation. We are saved by what our heart hears and believes, not our minds.

Here's how we can know if we are listening and believing with our heart or with our mind. When we believe something in our minds, it is comprised of thoughts and ideas that we hope are factual. This occurs when we have intellectually concluded something to be true.

Mentally, we can dissect every word in the Bible and still gain no understanding of it. This is because the Bible is not meant to be understood with our minds, but rather with our hearts. Look at this statement: *"For it is with your heart that you believe and are justified."* Head thoughts have no life or power connected to them. They are just notions of what is.

Our heart in the center of our created being, which means it is connected to God via His Spirit that He placed within us during our creation. When we believe from our heart, we believe from the place that God speaks to us.

Some say, "I need to get my mind right." I believe, however, that we need to get our heart right. Believing with our heart connects us to the Spirit of God.

My heart feels, expresses, perceives, and understands God better than my mind ever could. As psychology professor Robert Valett has said, "The human heart feels things the eyes cannot see, and knows things the mind cannot understand."[5] God's truths surpass the analytical workings of our minds and flow right to the heart.

Analytical thinkers crave data/information because they can process it. Heart people crave God because they trust Him more than they trust themselves. Our thoughts will never save us from anything.

Allow the presence of God to grow in your heart so that you can be saved and experience life in a whole new way.

This is a Thompson Truth!

---

5. https://allauthor.com/quotes/10826/

NOW, WRITE YOUR TRUTH:

_____

_____

_____

_____

_____

_____

_____

_____

_____

_____

_____

_____

_____

_____

_____

_____

No Faith in Faith

It appears that everywhere you look these days there are many who seem to have no faith in faith. Whether it's the idea of faith or the institutions of faith, there is no faith in faith.

Reports reflect that in 1980 more than 90% of Americans, or 204 million of the 227 million population, claimed to be Christian. Today, the population in America has risen to 332 million, with 65%, or 215 million, claiming to be

Christians. While the population grew by 105 million over those 40 years, there was a 25% decrease in the people of faith. Approximately 90 million people had less or no faith than those who did in 1980. What caused this? Allow me to share my thoughts on the subject.

We live in an extremely fast-paced society, where mostly everything can be received in an instant. We can get instant food, instant answers through the worldwide web, quick weight loss, instant tax refunds, instant credit, instant dating partners, etc. Everything is Click, Click, and Quick! However, faith is not like that, even though some have tried to make it seem so. Some contend that you can get whatever you want just by thinking about it: Blink, Think, Wink, and it's yours! Again, this is not true. Faith is a relationship, not a single act. Faith requires development through trust over time.

Even the disciples of Jesus, after seeing several miracles, as well as hearing countless testimonies, had no faith in faith. They saw what He did, but they had not experienced for themselves what He could do. Faith comes through experience. When something has not been experienced, it is tough to believe in it, and God has to be experienced, not just read about.

Faith should be viewed more like a relationship than a means to get something. God is not a genie. He is the

Person we are in the relationship with, and that relationship must be built on trust. *"How can two walk together unless there is a mutual agreement ... of trust."* God trusts that we will trust and follow Him ... no matter what things look like.

We can only see things from one angle/ perspective at a time, but God is multi-perspective. He sees from all perspectives at the same time. In other words, He is omniscient. God sees everything from all possible angles at the same time. Hence His ways are not like our ways. Here are some ways to build your faith relationship with the Person of God:

- Listen to God's Word – Find a way to hear the Bible read audibly to you.
- Trust God's Word – Accept/Believe

what you hear as the undeniable and irrefutable truth. Then, don't waiver!

• Apply the truth that you have heard and believed to your life.

Let's use Psalm 23 as our example: The Good Shepherd:

1. You, LORD, are my shepherd. I will never be in need.

APPLICATION: Lord God, I have chosen You as my Leader. I trust You to supply everything I need. I will keep the faith. I promise, no matter what. Amen!

2. You let me rest in fields of green grass. You lead me to streams of peaceful water.

APPLICATION: You know when I need rest and who I need rest from. I trust You to provide a peaceful place and time of needed rest for me. Amen!

> 3. And you refresh my life. You are true to your name, and you lead me along the right paths.

APPLICATION: I trust You! You won't lie to me. I can trust Your way of leading me, even when I don't understand it. Lead me, O Lord. Amen!

> 4. I may walk through valleys as dark as death, but I won't be afraid. You are with me, and your shepherd's rod makes me feel safe.

APPLICATION: I know it won't always be easy or feel good, but You will be there with me through it all. I have Your Word on that, and I trust Your Word. You will keep me safe. Amen!

5. You treat me to a feast, while my enemies watch. You honor me as your guest, and you fill my cup until it overflows.

APPLICATION: You will continue to provide for me, no matter what or who is in my life. You are my Provider. I will have more than enough because You are generous and loving to me. I believe that. Amen!

6. Your kindness and love will always be with me each day of my life, and I will live forever in your house, LORD.

APPLICATION: You will take care of me forever. You won't miss a day. I'm safe with You. I love You, Lord. Amen!

Listen, trust, apply! Listen, trust, apply! Listen, trust, apply! Have faith in faith.

This is a Thompson Truth!

NOW, WRITE YOUR TRUTH:

_____

_____

_____

_____

_____

_____

_____

_____

_____

_____

_____

_____

_____

_____

_____

_____

~27~

"Unblessable"

If we're being truly honest here, many of us, if not most or all of us, have felt "unblessable" at some point in our life. Our belief that we are "unblessable" is more of an indictment of ourselves than it is of God. We feel "unblessable" because we're unable, unsuitable, or unworthy to receive a blessing.

"Others are worthy and deserving of a blessing, but not me." This is what we tell ourselves. There are a few things we might feel we could possibly deserve, but other "stuff," the really big "stuff," no way!

Happiness, love, marriage, children, a great life, success, promotion, peace, stability, wealth are all things we feel were not meant for us. We feel wretched, unlucky, unfortunate, in need of punishment, or possibly even being outright damned. This is a self-damnation. Why? Because we feel "unblessable."

This a sentiment that we picked up somewhere, and we failed to put it back down. Maybe it was because of what some religious person said, or it could have been a family member, someone we admired, or someone we were in a relationship with. It's entirely possible that some random person off the streets planted that seed. Whoever it was, wherever it was, it made us feel as though we were or are "unblessable."

Sometimes the culprit is us. Why? Because we haven't forgiven ourselves for something that happened in the past. In some cases, it happened during our childhood. In other cases, it happened later in life. Either way, it's all lies. We are "blessable"! You are "blessable"! In fact, you are blessed! You've been blessed all along, and I want to prove it to you.

We live in a time and culture when everything is made to appear perfect. So, we strive to be a perfect person, a perfect parent, a perfect mate. We work hard to have a perfect body, live a perfect life, be a perfect Christian, be perfect at everything we do. Who is it who is spreading this narrative that we should be perfect? It is we people who are not perfect. God's Word says that no one is perfect, and yet He loves us.

We speak negatively about our weight, our looks, our intelligence, our race, and our pedigree, all because we have chosen to believe the lie that we are "unblessable. The truth is, we look like our heavenly Father, God. We were made in His image. So, let's start there and get rid of all the negative self-image talk.

God says that we were *"beautifully and wonderfully made."* Often the problem isn't what others think about us; it's what we think about ourselves. Far too often we compare ourselves to others whom we think have it all together. We need to stop putting down what were are not and start appreciating what we are. We must allow the wounds to heal from the arrows of insecurity.

Did you know that your self-image has a direct impact on your faith? Our feelings about ourselves affect our ability to receive God's promised blessings. He blessed His creation of humanity in Genesis, and we have been blessed ever since.

For those of you who might say, "Yeah, but I've been through some things since then," well, listen to this message that was shared with others who felt "unblessable." This message is entitled

"The Beatitudes," which is Latin for "The Blessings." As your read, keep in mind that the definition of the word *blessed* is "empowered to prosper":

> Empowered to prosper are those who feel unworthy, because the Kingdom of Heaven has been prepared especially for you.

The author could have stopped right there. That statement alone would have covered most of the folks hearing that message. But God always gives us more!

> Empowered to prosper are those who are hurting, for they shall be comforted.

Empowered to prosper are those who are meek and humble. Those who are willing to serve instead of demanding to be served. They will be richly provided for.

These are just the first three of the bessings/empowerments spoken regarding you and me. You can read them all for yourself in the Bible, in the books of Matthew (chapter 5) and Luke (chapter 6).

It's important that we hear our empowerment for ourselves. That way we can personally refute all lies.

Notice how the Beatitudes first tell how we feel about ourselves, then they share the truth of how God feels about us.

Clearly God has greater things planned for us all. We just have to learn to allow Him to have His way in our lives.

The next time someone tells you, "Have a blessed (empowered to prosper) day," tell them, "I will," and wish them the same. I wonder: what would happen if we began each day by declaring, "I have been empowered to prosper?" Maybe that's the BeOurAtitude!

This is a Thompson Truth!

NOW, WRITE YOUR TRUTH:

_____

_____

_____

_____

_____

_____

_____

_____

_____

_____

_____

_____

_____

_____

_____

_____

_____

_____

_____

28

"Churchism" or Church?

Today I want us to talk about the Church, like so many other people are already doing. Some say good things when talking about the Church; others say bad things. Many believe they have a good idea of what the Church is and isn't. The truth is that many really don't know.

What is the Church? Where is the Church? Who is the Church? Why is the Church? Most people's ideas have been formed by religion, history, hurts, tradition, and society. Some think the Church is a special building or place where Christians go to worship God on Sundays. Others think the Church is an organization of people who are brainwashed by the teachings of a mythical Jesus. Still others think it's just an event hall to do charitable works to get into Heaven, host politicians and Bingo Night. Lastly, there are those who believe the Church is a daytime nightclub for hypocrites, who condemn people everywhere to Hell, while being themselves some of the biggest hellions and chief sinners that have ever existed.

Some might be talking about *a* church, but certainly not *the* Church. Most folks are more familiar with "churchism." To really understand what the Church is we need to go to God to see what He says about it. After all, it is His Church that everyone wants to talk about.

Biblically speaking, the Church is not a building at all. Long before there ever was a building, followers of God had church in a tent or out in the open air somewhere, or in their own houses. God didn't sanction a huge edifice that men could boast about and use to inflict classism.

The actual first Church was the Garden of Eden, where everyone gathered. No labels! No dress codes! Just come as you are.

The Greek word translated to English as *church* is *ekklesia*, which means "the gathering." Adam was the first preacher,

Eve was the first lady, and the animals were the first congregants. The honored member and Head of the Church was God Himself. God and His gathering are what make up the true Church.

The purpose for the gathering/the Church is to honor God, not a man, nor a band, and not to grandstand. It's just for God. As we honor God, He loves on us, blesses us, and cares for us. That's what the gathering is for. When we go for the other "stuff," it's called "churchism," not Church.

God's Word speaks of those who reflect a form of godliness and power, while denying the authority behind the power. That is "churchism"! "Churchism" occurs when people come for the show at the gathering, rather than spending time with God, the Head of the gathering. "Churchism" seeks to separate people into a religious subculture, otherwise known as a denomination, and is associated with dogmatic emphasis on one thing or another. *Denominate* means "to divide, to place a value on one thing over another, one group over another group, one person over another person."

Some sprinkle, while others dunk. In some, no women preachers are allowed, while in others, whoever God calls can preach. Some wear makeup, but others consider it to be "of the devil." Some use only the King James Version of the Bible, and others have their preferred versions. And on and on it goes. Blah, blah, blah, and blah! What does it all lead to?

These are all various examples of denominations that "churchism" uses to divide us. Some people look at church as either or, all or nothing, perfect or hypocritical. But how can any group of humans be perfect? The answer, of course, is that they can't. That's why they need to be in the presence of a Holy God, who will help them overcome their issues and truly love one another and themselves.

You and I can reject that subculture and love the honored member and Head of the Church, our heavenly Father. Why don't we abandon the dogma, fear, and shaming, reject the pious meetings, money grabs, and masks, and leave the theatrics, gloating, and condemning behind? I'm not advocating leaving the Church; I'm saying we should leave the foolishness of man, the ways of "churchism."

God is the only pure truth there is in life. No one loves us more than He does. Why would we ever think about leaving Him?

If the pandemic has taught us anything, it has taught us all that we need to have our own personal relationship with God. But we also need the Church, the gathering with God and His angels. We all need more of God in our life!

Please don't let anything any man does turn you against God, and don't buy into all the shenanigans surrounding the things of God. Instead, let us gather as one, two, or a few, always allowing God to be the Head of our meetings, as well as the Head of our lives.

Granted, this message won't make people stop talking about the Church, but at least you and I will know the truth. God is in the Church. So, the next time someone asks, "Who's church do you attend," just smile and say, "God's."

This is a Thompson Truth!

NOW, WRITE YOUR TRUTH:

_____

_____

_____

_____

_____

_____

_____

_____

_____

_____

_____

_____

_____

_____

_____

_____

_____

29

God's Language

In one of my podcasts, I asked the question: "Why do we humans, the only ones of God's many creations, have a mouth to speak and ears to hear?"[6] The answer is because we are the only ones of God's many creations that were created in His image. Everything else God created was according to its own nature, but we were created according to the nature of God, nature being

6. I invite you to view "Mouth Almighty" on my site www.bentonthompsoniii.com/thompsontruths

characteristics, likeness. This was done with intentionality and purpose, which is to say that we were purposefully made to be like God.

Let's just sit on that statement for a moment … You and I were made to be like God! Since He is a speaking God, it makes sense that we would also speak. We can speak and hear what we speak because He can speak and hear what He speaks.

As children, we say the things we hear our parents say, whether curse words, expressions, salutations, greetings, judgements, or jokes. Whatever they say we say. Further, we say it like they say it. French-speaking parents have children who speak French. Maybe they also speak other languages, but they usually speak

French. Spanish-speaking parents and their children speak the same language. When parents speak Mandarin, their children do likewise.

This is true of every language and tongue that exists. Children speak their parents' language. Adam spoke the language of his Father, God, which begs the question: What is the language of God? Here is what I have found in my studies.

God's language commands millions and millions of angels to do as He says. Why? Because there is an irresistible, supernatural, limitless power in the language of God. Everything and everyone that has ever existed responds to God's language.

Since God is all powerful, it certainly stands to reason that so, too, is His language.

When I am speaking about the language of God, don't get it confused with the language of men. I'm not talking about whether God spoke Aramaic or Hebrew. The language of God is authentic to Him and who He is.

God's language is transcendent, translucent, and transformative. His language changes things from horrible to wonderful. All His children should be speaking His language.

Do you want to know what God's language is? It is the Word of God. The King James Version, New International Version, Amplified and Message Bible

Versions are all like dialects of God's language. No matter how it is said, it is still His language, His Word.

When we speak God's language, which is His Holy Word, great things happen. Blinded eyes open, diseases are healed, enemies wither, favor abounds, blessings erupt. When angels hear us saying, "Father God, thank You that no evil can come to me, nor can any plague come near my house," they immediately spring into action because they know we are speaking God's language, and they heed His voice.

Daniel prayed God's language/God's Word, and angels fought demons on his behalf. Hezekiah prayed God's language/ God's Word, and angels killed 185,000 enemy soldiers for him. Jairus prayed God's language/God's Word, and his daughter was brought back from the dead.

I wonder what could happen for us if we spoke God's language/the Word of God? In case you don't know what to say, just say, "Jesus." He is the Word of God!

This is a Thompson Truth!

NOW, WRITE YOUR TRUTH:

_____

_____

_____

_____

_____

_____

_____

_____

_____

_____

_____

_____

_____

_____

_____

_____

~30~

Doubting Builds Faith

Many of us have been led to believe that if you have faith, then you won't doubt. Or, if you really believed, your faith would never be swayed. Some say that true faith should always be unquestioning. We're told that you doubt because you have abandoned your faith, that faith and doubt are exact opposites, that doubt is the antithesis of faith.

It's true that you don't doubt what you know, but what did you do before you

235

knew? For many, it's as clear as black versus white. Either you have faith or you're a doubter.

But how does faith begin? Does it just happen suddenly for no reason? Does it just manifest out of thin air? Is there no rhyme or reason in how to get it? Is it magic? Is it only for a select few, the religious aristocracy?

Quite frequently, the faith we have originated from a doubt we used to have. Therefore, one could say that doubting is an essential part of having or getting faith, or, simply, that doubting builds faith.

Every faith giant that you can read about was formerly a doubter. It's an exception to wake up with faith about something that you haven't had any experiences with. It can happen, but it is rare. For most, having and getting faith is a process, a process that begins with doubting.

Without doubt, faith would not be faith. Doubt is what requires you to have faith. Doubt and faith are two sides of the same coin. Both are present.

Our doubts, when proven incorrect, are what cause us to have faith to believe. Again, this leads us to contend that doubting builds faith, just as challenges build character.

Many believe that doubting is the opposite of faith. That's not accurate. The true opposite of faith is certainty. Where certainty exists, you don't need faith. Doubting leads to questioning, questioning leads to testing, and testing leads to certainty. Testing your product before dispensing it is always a good idea. Make sure you believe what you say you believe before you say you believe it.

Some believe that doubt harms faith. Doubting nor having faith is the end of a matter. Faith, if followed out, could lead to believing. Or it might not. Doubt, if followed out, could also lead to believing. Or it might not.

Having faith doesn't mean you believe; it means you desire to believe. Doubt doesn't mean you don't believe; it means you are questioning what you believe.

Doubting and unbelieving are not the same thing. God doesn't reject doubters;

He welcomes them. He knows we all have questions.

The issue isn't doubting; it's what we do with our doubts. Our doubts can help increase our faith, just as the flu shot contains some of the virus that will help you fight it.

Allow your doubt to inoculate your faith and make you stronger and healthier. Every "faither" started out as a doubter. May you be the next "faither!"

This is a Thompson Truth!

NOW, WRITE YOUR TRUTH:

_____

_____

_____

_____

_____

_____

_____

_____

_____

_____

_____

_____

_____

_____

_____

_____

31

Everything Happens for a Reason

I would imagine that most, if not all, of us have heard or used the expression, "Everything happens for a reason." Generally, this phrase is used when something unexpected, bad, or confusing happens. We don't know what to say, or we can't explain what just happened, so we just say, "Everything happens for a reason."

This reminds me of another popular saying, "It is what it is." All too often this phrase is used when we don't know what else to say. "It is what it is," but do we know why it is?

Yes, everything happens for a reason, but do we know the reason? It's kind of like being given an equation to solve, and the answer you get or give is that math can be quite tricky. While being true, it doesn't answer the equation you were given.

We might believe there is a reason, but we don't know where or how to look for it. Well, today I want to attempt to provide a template to use to answer such equations.

We've all had bad, unforeseen, or puzzling things happen to us. Sometimes there is a tendency to try to compensate for things we don't understand. By compensate, I mean to ignore, or try and cover it up. We might not realize that the message is inside the mess that is before us. So, when we want to quickly rid ourselves of the mess, we miss the message that was contained therein.

Your mess, my mess, has an encrypted message, aka answer, inside of it. Only we can see it. Others can't fully see it for us. They can help us, but we must get the message for ourselves.

The reason we have not been able to solve those puzzling equations in life is because we are using the wrong formula. We try to figure out everything for ourselves. In doing so, we use past experiences, past lessons, folks we trust, and podcasts we've heard. All these things are knowledge-based, and knowledge cannot solve life's equations.

Knowledge is unilateral, but these equations are universal. Knowledge is flat, sequential, and horizontal in its progressions. In other words, you only know something after you have gone through it. We aren't using the correct tool for the job. Knowledge comes later in the game.

We need something to assist us while things are yet happening in our lives. We need wisdom! Wisdom is vertical in its progressions, always ascending. Wisdom elevates us to a level where we can see over the obstacles, unlike knowledge, which is horizontal and flat. Knowledge only sees the next challenge, not the next answer.

How do I get wisdom? I'm so glad you asked. Only God can give us wisdom. We know the WHAT, but only God knows the WHY. God said that if anyone wants wisdom, he or she should just ask Him for it, and He said He will give us as much as we need.

There are two key lessons I've learned here:

1. Ask God when you are ready and open to hear what He has to say.
2. The information you will receive may seem unconventional, weird, or quirky.

God's Word says that His ways are not like our ways. Expect something different.

So, the next time something happens that you didn't expect and that made you feel sad or confused, don't just say, "Everything happens for a reason." Ask God for wisdom to understand the message in the mess.

This is a Thompson Truth!

NOW, WRITE YOUR TRUTH:

_____

_____

_____

_____

_____

_____

_____

_____

_____

_____

_____

_____

_____

_____

_____

_____

_____

_____

_____

32

Everything Happens for a Season

In the last chat, we talked about the commonly used phrase, "Everything happens for a reason." In this chat, I want to deal with the not-as-famous counterpart—"Everything happens for a season." We all agree that everything happens for a reason, but the reason is because it's the season for it to happen. Hence, everything happens for a season.

King Solomon was one of the wisest men to have ever lived. He said, *"There is a season and a time appointed for everything under God's Heaven, a time for birth and a time for death, a time of war, a time of peace,"* etc. Every season is a season of change. It's rather like the seasons of the year.

Each season has its own importance, character, markings, and relevance. Each season brings a change in our life. Some are subtle and others not so subtle. Some seasons bring happiness, others sadness, some motivation, others listlessness. Some seasons cause pain, while some bring peace. All of them are needed and important. Different seasons yield different things, and to everything there is a season.

Seasons are not by luck, accident, or for punishment. They're by divine Providence. When we learn how to properly look, we can then see the hand of God in every season.

Spring moments are when things seem to burst open. New blooms and new beginnings, new relationships, new opportunities, new faces, new "stuff." *"Behold, all things are new!"*

Summer moments are beloved by many, a time when things are easy and carefree. There are no hard lessons to be learned, no teaching going on, and definitely no schooling.

Then comes the fall or autumn moments. It's harvest time, when all your hard work finally pays off. Things look bright and colorful. Vibrancy is everywhere.

We all have winter moments, time to store up, hunker down, get cozy, and rejuvenate.

These all might be things we see in the seasons, but why do they come? King Solomon also stated that every season has a purpose.

Why, in that autumn, did I have to lose a leaf off my family tree? It was for new growth to come forth, to produce a new bud and a new bloom.

Why was that such a cold, icy, and bitter wintertime in my life? It was to kill and break off that which would have made you bitter.

Why did it have to get so hot and uncomfortable in that situation? It was to wither and shrivel up some things that needed to stop growing in your life.

Why did so many tears have to drop like rain? It was to wash away all the debris that was starting to pile up around you.

To every season, there is a purpose, and the purpose for the season is transition. Life must not remain static. You and I must not remain static. No matter how good or how bad our current situation, nothing can remain the same forever. Transition is inevitable and even needed.

In the transitions, we learn to handle the horrible "stuff," the bad turns to good, and the good turns to better.

Each transition presents us with the benefits of a brand-new season. God promises us that for every death, there is a new life awaiting us. Maybe it's our own. Maybe it's someone we had not previously seen before. Everyone likes new beginnings, but old things must end before the new can begin.

I like a harvest. I also like to dig, get dirty, work long hours, plant, and tend a field, as well as spend my money for the seeds. You cannot have a harvest without all the rest.

God's purpose for every season of transition is to keep us growing. We must look beyond the experience, to learn from its significance. When things change, we grow. We go from being battle weary to being battle tested.

That sickness is being used to build a better immune system. Those hurts will be used to help others. We are no longer victims; we have become victors.

Every change presents a choice. Stand and grow now or run away and have to face it again. Everything is working for our good. Therefore, embrace the season. Embrace the transition. Embrace the growth.

What we have gone through has taught us how to go through. And happiness has greater value for those of us who have been hurt. We must thank God for this season we are in now and ask Him to teach us its significance!

This is a Thompson Truth!

NOW, WRITE YOUR TRUTH:

_____

_____

_____

_____

_____

_____

_____

_____

_____

_____

_____

_____

_____

_____

_____

_____

33

Networking and Connections

Networking is a term that most of us are very familiar with. It's been around for quite some time now, since the 1960s, to be exact.

We all know about trying to make the right connections. Whether for business or personal life, everyone's looking for the right hook-ups. We can all use some help in life.

We're trying to connect with the right manager, the person who is the influencer, the individual who suits us best, the one who will be right for us. We attend dinners, benefits, and gatherings, we use social media, join organizations, exchange cards and numbers, and seek updated contact information. But how many times has our brilliant plan failed? There was no success the first time we tried it, the fifth time we tried it, nor the fiftieth time we tried it. Where has social networking gotten us?

We believe that the more we're out there the better our chances are to find what we want or need. So, we search profiles, pages, accounts, IGs, etc., and ask folks about other folks, trying to naturally connect with those who have what we think we want and/or need.

We feel these relationships would be very convenient for us if we could just connect. After all, it would stand to reason that since we like similar things, we must be similar people, right?

Sadly, I have discovered that it's not necessarily true. While our likes may be similar, our motivation could be different. Very often, our real need is much deeper than the "stuff" we want and seek.

In truth, we are seeking a closeness, a kindred soul, folks who are like us at their core, like-minded and like-spirited, cut from the same cloth, as it were.

I read in my faith manual where God said it is both good and sweet when you are unified and surrounded by those who share your same values. I couldn't agree more. We've been looking for convenient connections; God has divine connections, good and sweet connections with like-spirited and like-minded folks.

It is great to work, fellowship, live, play, hang out, or do business with those with whom God has constructed a divine connection for us, and He has those divine connections for all of us. Such divine connections come through spiritual networking. As it turns out, networking is just a fancy way of saying "work on building a relationship."

As we work on building our relationship with God spiritually, He will begin to connect us with others who are like us. That's what spiritual networking is all about. God has divine connections lined up for each of us, and they are all over the place, folks who will assist us in getting where we need to be.

Divine connections release power in your life, as well as the lives of those with whom you are connected. There is an awesome energy that flows through you when you are in a divine connection.

Sometimes we will have to overcome barriers to get in that divine connection, barriers of our past, barriers of our mind, barriers of pride, barriers of prejudice, barriers of prior relationships, and all that we "know." But don't worry! God will see you through it. He promises that we will fulfill our destiny. Grow in your communication with God, and you will see your divine connections coming to life.

This is a Thompson Truth!

NOW, WRITE YOUR TRUTH:

_____

_____

_____

_____

_____

_____

_____

_____

_____

_____

_____

_____

_____

_____

_____

~34~

Anomalous Insight

If you were someone who had anomalous insight, you would be like a modern-day superhero. We all know that every superhero has a superpower. Wonder Woman has her belt of truth, Spider Man has his "spidey senses," and Superman has his superhuman strength. Your superpower would be anomalous insight.

I'm not talking about your standard or normal insight. It would be

263

extraordinary—extra ordinary. You would have something like x-ray vision insight. I call it x-ray analytics. You would have a deeper view through the window of insight into a situation. You would know things that you could not naturally know.

There is a company in New York that is called Anomaly Insights, and they use artificial intelligence to gain insight to help improve healthcare quality. But you and I can do better than artificial intelligence; we have divine intelligence.

Robots don't know what God knows. God is all knowing; robots have to be programmed. The Great Divine has made available to us anomalous insight. Through wisdom, which is a superpower, we can all receive anomalous insight.

The great King Solomon received wisdom from God. He had everything a person could want, but he didn't know the why of things. Simply put, he had no insight. He lacked understanding. Solomon wanted anomalous insight, so he asked God, and he received what he had asked for.

We all have choices to make, and we could all use better insight to enable us to make better choices. Some choices come hourly, some come daily, and others come at various intervals throughout life. If you're like me, you've made some good choices, and some not-so-good choices. We hope and pray that our good choices outweigh our bad ones. I know for sure that all my bad choices were made when I did not seek God enough for His wisdom.

The gift of anomalous insight would not only benefit us, but also those around us. Many times, the personal choices we make can also affect and influence others. "It's my career, but my choices still might affect others." "It's my body, but … ." "It's my life, but … ." It's my whatever, but … !"

As the king, Solomon knew that his decisions would not only affect him, but also many others around him. He viewed it as being irresponsible to those whom he had a responsibility for, to not seek wisdom to be a better leader. And I tend to agree with him. We need wisdom for ourselves, but even more so if we have a responsibility for anyone else. Our lives are often interconnected with others.

Solomon knew that sooner or later he would need anomalous insight to guide him through a situation that involved someone else, and one day that situation came in the form of a dispute that he would have to settle. This situation had been considered by others, but no one knew what to do, so they brought it to the king.

The situation was this: Two different women were pregnant and delivered their babies a few days apart. Both ladies were said to be prostitutes and lived in the same bordello. One of the babies died, and when it happened, that mother quickly exchanged her dead baby for the living baby. Then, each woman claimed she was the mother of the living baby. Unfortunately, both ladies' credibility was questionable, and so the matter was deferred to the king for his decision.

If Solomon ever needed anomalous insight, it was now. Imagine the range of human emotions for the mother whose child was taken. Get this decision wrong, and there would be long-lasting ramifications.

After hearing both sides, Solomon made his decision, and it was based on anomalous insight. He demanded that the living baby be cut in half, right down the middle.

At first glance, that didn't seem like a wise decision at all. In fact, it seemed more cruel and inhumane than any other alternative. Why not insist on shared custody between the two women? Why not place the child as a ward of the State? Surely there had to be a better decision than to just kill the baby.

But Solomon had insight from God. He had his superpower. He wasn't relying on past experiences or a best guess. He was relying upon heavenly wisdom. He knew that the real mother of the child would never agree to his suggestion.

One of the women said, "Okay, go ahead. Do it," but the other woman wept bitterly and begged for the child's life, asking that he be spared and given to the other woman. Solomon knew that this was the true mother, for she would want her child alive at all costs.

Granted, maybe not all our decisions are life-altering like this one, but wouldn't it be great to have a superpower of anomalous insight at your availability?

The lesson learned here is this: See how wise we can be as humans, when we walk in wisdom and have anomalous insight given by God. Don't miss out on your superpower. Ask God to give you this gift today!

This is a Thompson Truth!

NOW, WRITE YOUR TRUTH:

_____
_____
_____
_____
_____
_____
_____
_____
_____
_____
_____
_____
_____
_____
_____
_____
_____
_____
_____
_____

35

Hindsight Foresight

I know this might sound like an oxymoron or double speak, but it's not. Follow along, and you'll see where I'm going with this.

Have you ever wished that you could have done something differently, sought out some advice, waited a bit longer, considered some other options, perhaps gone a different route, made a different choice, or not chosen at all?

What if you could have known then what you know now? Would you rethink that purchase? That relationship? That commitment? What if? That's the million-dollar question, isn't it? What if?

I'm not saying that we should cry over the spilled milk of yesterday or yesteryear. We did the best we could with what we knew. But what if we could have known more? What if we'd had hindsight foresight? Let's explore that a bit more, to gain some more understanding.

Hindsight is "the ability to understand and realize something about an event after it happened, something that you did not realize at the time." *Foresight* is "the power of foreseeing, the ability or result of an ability to use insight to predict what will happen in the future." If we could put those two things together, we could have a powerful force—Hindsight Foresight. Then we would know the answer to the great What If?

If I could have known and used then what I know now, that would be great. But how could we put those two together? I'm so glad you asked.

In the definition of *hindsight*, notice that it says that "you did not realize at the time." This infers that you could have realized it, but you didn't. In other words, it was realizable. We just didn't realize it or acknowledge it at the time. Hmmm!

Now, let's look at that word *foresight* again. *Foresight* speaks of "an ability to foresee," which means it is possible to foresee. We just need to tap into that ability to foresee, right? So, if you and I acknowledged that there could be another possible realization other than what we thought we knew and we were open and available to the ability to foresee, then we would foreknow.

Let's read that again, please. If you and I acknowledged that there could be another possible realization other than what we thought we knew and we were open and available to the ability to foresee, then we would foreknow. There's a lot of meat on that bone. We could stop right here and feast very well. With that thought in mind, this is a Thompson Truth. No, I'm just kidding! Let's walk a little further together.

All too often we are closed off and not predisposed to the idea of accepting or acknowledging anything other than what we have predetermined that we know. The thing that blocks us from acknowledging is in the very word I just used —*acknowledge*. Acknowledgment is our recognition of something that we have accepted as valid or legitimate. When we think we already know something, we are not open to the idea of knowing something else, because we have already accepted that which we know or think is proven to be accurate, valid, and legitimate.

We have said to ourselves, "There's no other truth than that which I already know, the truth that I have already accepted in my mind." We have thus convinced ourselves that our way is how it is, and so we know it!

In other words, this happens when we are not open and available to the ability to foresee something, anything, because we think we already know everything or at least what is to be known pertaining to this matter. Yes, we know what is known, but we don't know that which is unknown or not yet known.

The unknown is just unknown for now. That doesn't mean it can't be known. It is possible to know the unknown ... if we are willing to be open and make ourselves available to a different route and a different approach.

Here's some homework: Ask yourself a few telling questions:

- If I would have known differently, would I have chosen to accept it?
- Could I have gone another route, other than the one I deemed correct?
- Would I have only trusted what I had come to know for myself personally?
- Do I trust anyone or anything else other than myself?
- Do I trust God?
- Should I trust God?
- Can I trust God?

In another chat we will continue our conversation on the challenges of considering the known versus the unknown.

This is a Thompson Truth!

NOW, WRITE YOUR TRUTH:

_____

_____

_____

_____

_____

_____

_____

_____

_____

_____

_____

_____

_____

_____

_____

_____

36

Enigmatic Simplicity

In one of my podcasts, we referenced an enigma about a chicken and an egg. We related that to which came first, knowledge or wisdom? Feel free to refresh yourself by revisiting that message.[7]

The story of the Garden of Eden also has an enigma in it. In the garden, there were various kinds of trees, beautiful to the eye and good to eat. In the middle of the garden, there was a very different

7. I invite you to view "Knowledge or Wisdom" on my site www.bentonthompsoniii.com/thompsontruths

kind of tree. It was called the Tree of Life. Another tree of notoriety located near this one was called the Tree of the Knowledge of Good and Evil. Both trees were quite exquisite and unique.

Adam was told that he could freely eat from all the trees in the garden, except for the Tree of the Knowledge of Good and Evil. God said, *"Don't eat from it. The moment you eat from that tree, you're dead."*

As we know, Adam and Eve both ate from the Tree of Knowledge of Good and Evil, yet they did not physically die. What, then, did God mean when he told Adam, "If you eat from it, you're dead?" Therein lies the enigma. Is knowledge the forbidden fruit or does it deliver on its promise to unlock the mysteries we seek the answers to? That is the question at hand.

Which of the two options would you have chosen: the Tree of Knowledge or the Tree of Life? Even today, this is still a choice set before us. Life or knowledge, which should I choose? Do I just keep living my life without regard for anything or anyone else, without concern for consequence or significance, carefree, with meaningless immortality, tumbling through time, day after day? Or do I try to get as much knowledge as I possibly can in the hope that it will help me navigate better through life? Is it true that the more I know the better off I'll be? Shouldn't I have an opportunity to choose for myself, whether right or wrong? I want to make my own choices. I don't trust anyone to choose for me.

Which would you choose? Perhaps since getting knowledge wasn't really the death of Adam, maybe you'd choose that path. Maybe you can get all the knowledge you need to make it. After all, Adam survived!

Others might consider the carefree life path option. Do what you want when you want with no accountability, no one to answer to, no one to boss you around! "I am the boss of me!"

Which is the best choice? We can't have both, so we must choose. Unfortunately, far too often we have chosen that forbidden path. Whether the enemy beguiled me or the inner me beguiled me, I can't be sure.

Sometimes the best answer is the simplest answer. Enigmatic, yes, but that doesn't mean the answer is not simple. Sometimes we overcomplicate by overthinking a matter.

I personally would choose the other option presented before these two. "What other option?" you might ask. "Did I miss something here?" I would choose the first option, Adam's life before, before he exercised his option to choose for himself.

In the beginning, when Adam was formed from the earth, God breathed life into him, and he became a living soul. God put His arms around Adam, held him close, and resuscitated him. God gave him spiritual CPR or a parturition of spirit.[8]

---

8. View my podcast, "Parturition of Spirit," at:
   www.bentonthompsoniii.com/thompsontruths

This means that prior to this interaction with God, Adam was a dead soul. As a result of God initiating their relationship, Adam now had life. He could see. He could sense. He could discern.

God and Adam would spend several hours together walking and talking in the garden. Adam was naked and transparent. No lies! No masks! No agendas! No pretenses! Their fellowship time was so sweet, so personal, and so private. Every day, all day, just the two of them. Wow! One could only imagine the things they must have talked about.

When God told Adam that if he ate from the Tree of the Knowledge of Good and Evil he would be dead, notice that He didn't say that Adam would die; He said he would be dead.

As a result of Adam's choice, he and his wife were evicted from Paradise, and he was relegated to a life of back-breaking labor. Plus, he and Eve were now homeless. Even though these were bad things, there was not the death that God had spoken of.

Perhaps the worst result of their disobedience was that they lost the precious fellowship they had enjoyed with God. Prior to Adam's decision to eat from the tree, he had walked with God (aka Wisdom, aka The Ancient of Days) every day. He was receiving wisdom and insight on a regular basis. So, his eating from the Tree of Knowledge did represent a death, a death to the wisdom that he had been receiving daily, a death to his closeness with God, a death to living life as he had once known it.

Adam ended this daily communion because of his thirst for knowledge. He just wanted to know more. What could be wrong with that? Knowledge is knowing, but wisdom is knowing what to do with what you know. Now that we know, do we know what to do with what we know?

Adam forsook wisdom for knowledge. He missed the part about making wise choices versus unwise choices. He didn't know what to do with what he had. By what he suffered, Adam learned that a relationship with God is better than all the knowledge in the world.

We need to thank the first Adam for providing us with his wisdom and experience, and we need to thank the ultimate and last Adam for providing us new life. *"The first man, Adam, became a living being; the last Adam became a life-giving spirit."*

Now we can go outside, in nature, in the garden, and God will be waiting there for us again, ready to walk and talk with us, just like in the beginning. He will give us wisdom because He is the Ancient of Days.

So, go outside somewhere after receiving this message. God is waiting for you there!

This is a Thompson Truth!

NOW, WRITE YOUR TRUTH:

_____

_____

_____

_____

_____

_____

_____

_____

_____

_____

_____

_____

_____

_____

_____

_____

37

Keen Percipience

When I wrote this at the beginning of a new year, my intent was not necessarily to share a new message, but rather to give us new purpose and new intentionality.

Over the next few weeks, I shared various truths that I had received concerning wisdom. First, we looked at what we can have, learning to understand the value of wisdom and how it is the most desired treasure of all treasures. I called this chat "Inestimable Wealth."[9]

9. I invite you to view the complete podcast at

Next, we looked at what we can become, how we can all be superheros by using the superpower of wisdom, to change not only our own life, but also the lives of those around us. I called this chat "Anomalous Insight."[10]

After that, we looked at What If? If I knew better, I could do better. If I knew then what I know now, I might have made better decisions. We learned that the unknown can be known, if we just tune into it. I called this chat "Hindsight Foresight."[11]

Then, we looked at why we need wisdom. It is to help us break bad habits

---

www.bentonthompsoniii.com/thompsontruths

10. I invite you to view the complete podcast at
www.bentonthompsoniii.com/thompsontruths.

11. I invite you to view the complete podcast at
www.bentonthompsoniii.com/thompsontruths

and not continually operate in hindsight bias. Wash! Rinse! Repeat! Wash! Rinse! Repeat! I called this chat "Knowledge or Wisdom?"[12]

At the very core of my soul, I am a pragmatic learner, as are most seekers of the truth. We look for ways to apply the lessons we've learned to our personal lives. In this information age in which we live, it is very easy to become a data glut. "Gimmie, Gimmie, Gimmie! My name is Jimmy, and I'll take all the information you can gimmie." Well, my name is not Jimmy, and I am not someone who just wants information.

It's dangerous to receive information faster than you can process it. You can get

---

12. I invite you to view the complete podcast at
www.bentonthompsoniii.com/thompsontruths

intellectual heartburn, mental angina, or become an intelligent idiot. These things happen when we don't take the time to digest what we are eating.

I share truths with other pragmatics like myself, also known as seekers. We pragmatics can handle something even if it doesn't make sense to us right now. We know that we don't know all there is to know.

But what we learn does have to have purpose. We must be able to use what we've learned. We use information to help us make decisions to take actions that are useful in practice, not just in theory.

We're not seeking to be religious, but rather to be relational. How can I relate to what is being said to me? Trivia is trivial.

In this chat, we will look at the practicality of wisdom and how it can help us to have keen percipience.

Wisdom is a rare commodity. One can easily increase in knowledge or learning. We can store up knowledge through books, research, and education. But to acquire wisdom the process is a little different, not necessarily harder, just different.

To receive wisdom you must be willing to sacrifice your knowledge. I must be willing to put aside what I know (or what I think I know) to acquire the wisdom that I must have.

After all, it was our own knowledge, that got us into the binds that we have gotten into in the first place. I, for one, am certainly willing to trade in my knowledge for God's wisdom.

Some might ask, "What can wisdom do for me?" Pragmatically speaking, wisdom will help us to have better judgment. Very often, our judgement of a person, situation, or subject is off. Our percipience needs to be adjusted. It is not keen. And when our percipience is off, that's how we miss our blessings. That's why we need keen percipience.

Look at what this beautiful proverb has to say:

"Learn to become wise and develop good judgement and good common sense! This point cannot be overemphasized. As you cling to wisdom, she will protect you. Love

her, and she will guard you. Getting wisdom is the most important thing you can do. And with wisdom comes the development of common sense and good judgement. If you value and uphold wisdom, she will value and uphold you. Hold her close and tight to you, and she will lead you to great honor. She will place a beautiful crown upon your head."

Wow, what a powerful and beautiful proverb about wisdom! Notice that the proverb refers to wisdom as "she," sensitive, caring, and nurturing. Love her and honor her—the beautiful lady wisdom—and as we do so, we will get in return good judgement and good common sense.

Now that's exactly what we pragmatic learners need, not okay percipience, but keen percipience, percipience that is good and practical, not my judgment, but God's good judgement. I'm in! Would you care to join me?

This is a Thompson Truth!

NOW, WRITE YOUR TRUTH:

_____

_____

_____

_____

_____

_____

_____

_____

_____

_____

_____

_____

_____

_____

_____

_____

_____

_____

_____

38

Knowledge or Wisdom?

If you had to choose to have either knowledge or wisdom, which one would it be? There are plenty of good arguments on both sides. Both are good, but what if you could only choose one?

Many people believe that you can gain wisdom through the knowledge that you have about a particular situation or circumstance. It is possible to gain a little wisdom through your personal knowledge. However, it is not guaranteed.

That is why many times we repeat some of the same mistakes over and over again. It's like the ever-popular saying: Wash! Rinse! Repeat! Wash! Rinse!Repeat!

The little knowledge that we have gained is hindsight from a previous experience. Therefore, the knowledge we think could be considered wisdom only applies to a situation exactly like the one we just experienced. Rarely do we have a repeat of the exact same situation or circumstance. Usually there is something or someone different involved in the next experience. So, then, rarely is the wisdom we gained from any past knowledge applicable going forward. In other words, you can only use what you have learned in a particular situation.

More often than not, we end up with hindsight bias. Hindsight bias is when we think we know everything, based solely upon the things we have already experienced. Unfortunately, we find ourselves in a constant cycle of repeating mistakes, not having learned the necessary lessons, and surely not changing our methods.

In one of my podcasts, I shared a Thompson Truth I called "Living Looking Back."[13] Check it out to hear more. There are some lessons to be learned from our previous mistakes. As they say, "Live and learn!"

The little knowledge we have gained will prove to be insufficient for our future.

13. I invite you to view the entire podcast at:
    www.bentonthompsoniii.com/thompsontruths

We must ask ourselves: Is knowledge the chicken or the egg? Do I know because I am wise? Or am I wise because I know? Knowledge is what comes from your own understanding. Wisdom is what comes from trusting the understanding of another.

Knowledge says, "Ahh, now I know." Wisdom says, "There is much more to be known." Knowledge can be arrogant and cocky; wisdom is humble and open. Knowledge can make one quick to move, because they believe they know the way. Wisdom will cause you to move slower, because you realize you are still being shown the way.

A knowledgeable person is not always a wise person, but a wise person certainly has acquired a lot of knowledge. There is a proverb that states the following:

"Trust in and rely confidently on God with all your heart. And do not rely on your own insight or understanding. In everything that you do acknowledge/seek out God first. And he will smooth things out for you, and remove obstacles that block your way."

We go off of what we know, not what we could have known. What we could have known comes from wisdom. And hindsight foresight wisdom comes from God. What are some things that you would ask God for wisdom on? Well, go ahead! Ask Him now! There is no time like the present. We have gone long enough without wisdom!

This is a Thompson Truth!

NOW, WRITE YOUR TRUTH:

_____

_____

_____

_____

_____

_____

_____

_____

_____

_____

_____

_____

_____

_____

_____

~39~

Parturition of Spirit

Wisdom is a rare commodity, and not just everyone has it. This is not because there is a limited supply or low availability. Quite the opposite is true. There is an unlimited supply of all the wisdom we would ever need.

Wisdom is rare because it has exceptional beauty, with value unlike anything else, but it is uniquely acquired. One can easily increase in knowledge or learning. We can store up knowledge through books, research, and education. But to acquire wisdom the process is a little different, not harder, just different. In this chat, let's explore what different looks like.

As previously stated, to receive wisdom we must be willing to sacrifice our knowledge. We must be willing to put aside what we know or what we think we know to acquire the wisdom that we must have. Knowledge is a natural process that is birthed and resides in the region of the mind. Wisdom is a process imbedded and made alive in one's spirit. That is why we need a parturition of spirit. Like water during birth, parturition of spirit will dictate the timing, and we must go with the flow.

The deeper meaning of wisdom is "the ability to distinguish that which is wise from that which is unwise." The best way to become wise is by intentionally cultivating your relationship with wisdom. Therein lies the key. Wisdom is relational, and knowledge is impersonal. You don't need to have a relationship with anyone to become knowledgeable. You can read and study all on your own, never interacting with anyone.

Wisdom is different. It is all about relationship. You learn and grow in wisdom from your relationships with others. I've heard it said: "Wisdom provides a level of knowledge that is above college." Many great leaders and influencers have had mentors to learn from, someone from whom they could gain insight and feedback. They were provided wisdom from the learnings of others.

If we want to follow the example of another, we should look for someone to instruct us who has sound wisdom, someone we deem to be wise. Once we have identified that person, we should spend dedicated time with them and allow them to share their learnings with us.

It is extremely important that we choose the right guide. We are not looking for someone who only has knowledge. We want someone who walks, lives, and breathes wisdom. If that sounds like a tall order to fill, it's because it is.

People are fickle, as we know all too well. One minute we do, and the next we don't. But do you know who is always constant and stable? God. He never changes, which means He never gets old and forgets. He is always current and relevant. He knows our past and our future.

All the wisdom I have I have received from my relationship with God. Notice I did not say from going to church. I said from my relationship with God. God is Wisdom. One of the other many names for God is Ancient of Days, which means He is All-Wise.

Wisdom is transmittable. When you hang out with God, you get wisdom by contact. Wisdom is not gotten *from*; it is gotten *by*, by fellowship with God.

Find a place where you can see nature. Go outside somewhere. Steal away from all the noise. Don't bring your phone, computer, or any other electronic device. Focus on the sky, a cloud, a tree, a bird, the wind, whatever you like, and just hang out there for a few minutes, watching, looking. You don't have to say anything. Just sit and listen, listen to wisdom from the Ancient of Days.

This is a Thompson Truth!

NOW, WRITE YOUR TRUTH:

_____

_____

_____

_____

_____

_____

_____

_____

_____

_____

_____

_____

_____

_____

_____

_____

_____

40

Brain Transplant

Transplanting is a medical procedure in which an organ is removed from one person's body and placed in the body of another. Organ transplanting has been accomplished by science with overall good results. Many lives have been extended because of this scientific development.

The list of successful organ transplants includes the heart, kidneys, lungs, pancreas, intestine, and uterus, just to name a few. There have also been advancements in transplanting bone, tissue, muscle, and other human elements. The first successful medically recorded heart transplant took place in 1967, and from there, great advances have been made. This is where my Medical PSA or Public Service Announcement ends.

But what about the brain? Can it be safely transplanted? Science has attempted to accomplish this feat as well, but the reported results have not been favorable. One of the greatest challenges in completing this procedure is the brain's connection to the spinal cord and the bundles of nerves that feed off from it. The same bundle of nerves that are in the ENS (the Enteric Nervous System).[14]

14. View the podcast entitled "Instinctual Acuity" at:

I'm not suggesting that we can get a brain transplant, but we do need an autotransplantation. The word *auto* is Greek for "self." Hence we need a transplant within ourselves. We need an autotransplantation. An autotransplantation is when an organ is moved from one part of a person's body to another part of their body. And I'm suggesting that the brain is the organ that needs to be moved. The brain, in the sense of the place where we process what actions we take.

Look at what a sacred writing said, *"Let this mind be in you, the same (mind) that was in Jesus."* How can we have a different mind than the one we've always had? Through autotransplantation! Simply put, we need to start thinking out of our heart, or spirit, instead of thinking out of our head. Then, when those unctions come to us out of our spirit, we must start obeying them.

Some of us are having an unction right now that we need to do something about. Do you feel it? It's there because we have a direct connection to God's Spirit through the spirit that He placed within us. This serves as our spiritual spinal cord. When we don't have regular fellowship time with God, we are in danger of damaging that spiritual spinal cord connection.

Research has shown that the heart is not just a muscle; it also contains independent memory. Once again scientist have proven what God has always known.

Look at Psalm 16:7. *"I will praise the LORD, who counsels me; even at night my heart instructs me."* Notice the words *"heart instructs me."* Our heart is speaking to us, but are we listening?

This is why we are awakened sometimes in what we call "the middle of the night." God is speaking to us through our heart, trying to instruct us about something or other. Here's a tip: Have some paper or a notebook and a pen handy by your bedside so that you can write down what you are hearing.

Information has been embedded in the cells in our body/heart from the beginning when God made Adam. God blew into Adam's Enteric Nervous System his own Deoxyribonucleic acid (DNA), and filled every cell in his body with wisdom, knowledge, power, and grace. As heirs of Adam, that same DNA still exists in us today.

Let us be warned that if we continue to disregard these nudges that we feel in our spirit (to do or not to do something) we can develop calluses, which will be spiritually unhealthy for us. If our heart forms calluses, this will inhibit our ability for the ear in our heart to hear God.

A callused heart is one that judges, won't forgive, won't submit, is prideful, arrogant, self-righteous, full of hatred, hurt, meanness, and envy, among other bad things. We know when our heart is not right. No one needs to tell us. If you've had this to happen, don't worry. God has a cure!

Here is a prayer we should pray every day. It will keep us from getting calluses. *"Create in me a pure heart, O God, and renew a steadfast spirit within me. Do not cast me from your presence or take your Holy Spirit from me. Restore to me the joy of your salvation and grant me a willing spirit, to sustain me"* (Psalm 51:10-12)

I pray that you will be heart healthy!

This is a Thompson Truth!

NOW, WRITE YOUR TRUTH:

_____

_____

_____

_____

_____

_____

_____

_____

_____

_____

_____

_____

_____

_____

_____

_____

41

Instinctual Acuity

You know when you get that funny sensation about something? You know the one I'm speaking of, when something just feels different. You can't quite put your finger on what it is, but it's there. You feel you know something about what is about to happen, but you don't know how you know it.

Maybe it's an event, a person, or a situation, and you just have a feeling about it. It doesn't necessarily have to be a bad sensation; you just feel something.

Sometimes it is a bad vibe, but at other times it might be a good one. We often call that our "gut instincts," or we say, "Something told me."

What would you say if I told you that you are correct on both accounts? Something did tell you, and it was your gut. Yes, your gut spoke to you. Deep within every human being, there is an instinctual acuity. It also has many other names, like "hunch," "instinct," "intuition," "sixth sense," and "discernment." These all add up to the same thing—a knowing without knowing how we know it.

Sometimes this can be a bother because we feel we must know everything. How?

Who? When? Where? Why? and What for? Not knowing can be unsettling, unless you are at a place where you realize you cannot possibly know everything.

Science has come to know and explain a lot of things that God has said were true, and instinctual acuity is one of the many things that science now understands. According to science, instinctual acuity takes place in the little or second brain. The second brain is in our ENS (Enteric Nervous System), or gut, as we know it.

The big or first brain, the one located in our skull, operates through our CNS (Central Nervous System) and that's where we formulate our thoughts. The second brain gathers insights and assessments that are provided from the spiritual/unseen realm and then sends those findings to the first or big brain. This explains why we don't know where the knowledge came from because we did not learn it in the conventional method.

You know it without knowing how you know it. Your ENS sent a backdoor message to your CNS. The message went something like this, "This is real, so don't ignore it!" The essence of your being spoke to the image of your being and told it what was real and true.

I know this is some heavy stuff, with first brain, second brain, and our gut speaking and all, but just try to finish the chat and hear the truth. Also, listen to the voice on the inside of you right now that is saying, "He's right!"

Our brain is the centerpiece of our CNS (Central Nervous System), and it contains half of our bodies nerve cells. Can you imagine where the other half of our nerve cells are located? Yes, in the gut. Our gut contains over 100 million neutrons/ nerves, which is far more than are in our spinal cord that serves as the lifeline to the brain.

Our gut is considered to be made up of those areas in our core, like the stomach, intestines, heart, kidneys, etc. We feel what we feel in our gut, not our brain. Also, contrary to what many believe, our brain does not determine whether we are happy or sad. Our gut does.

We experience sensations in our stomach, hair stands up on our arms or on the back of our necks, and, of course, we feel it in our heart, somewhere in our core. Our gut has a mind of its own. Our true identity is held in our core, aka our gut.

When God breathed His energy into man, He did it through the ENS (Enteric Nervous System), which is the esophagus, lungs, kidneys, and heart. That's why God tells us not to be nervous, because He gave us our nervous system.

Let's pause right here for a bit, so we can let that one soak in. God gave you and me the nerves to do what we must do. Into the bowels of man, God breathed some of Himself, and man became alive. Essentially, God placed His greatness within each of us, starting with Adam. This means that you are already great.

Why? Because God made you from the greatness in Himself.

All of us are composed of three parts: One part flesh (the dirt, earthy soil matter which Adam was prior to his encounter with God), one part spirit (which God imparted from Himself into Adam, and he became a living soul), and the last part is the soul, those things which we have learned or been taught to do in our minds. This is what makes up our whole being. This is who we are.

Those three parts are referred to as the body, spirit, and soul of man. If you are interested in learning more on this subject, I recommend my book *How to Hear God.*[15]

---

15. My books are all available on my site:
      www.bentonthompsoniii.com/shop

In upcoming Truths, we will be looking at learning how to tap into the power that God has placed within our core being. For now, just keep a journal of the things you have been feeling in your gut, not your brain (where thoughts can run rampant). Those things you feel in the very core of your being are spot on. I have a gut feeling that you will find those things to be very helpful very soon!

This is a Thompson Truth!

NOW, WRITE YOUR TRUTH:

_____

_____

_____

_____

_____

_____

_____

_____

_____

_____

_____

_____

_____

_____

_____

_____

_____

42

Trusting Our Gut

As noted in another chat, all of us have instinctual acuity. According to science, instinctual acuity takes place in the little or second brain. The second brain is in our ENS (Enteric Nervous System), or gut, as we know it. We feel what we feel in our gut, not in our brain. That's where we get the phrase, "Something told me." So why not trust our gut?

When we get that feeling in our gut, that something is going on, we know it's right.

We know we should listen to it. We know we should go with what it is telling us. When we don't do it, we end up regretting that we didn't trust our gut.

Probably right now, many of us are reflecting on some times when we didn't trust our gut, those times we wished we would have done differently, and because of it, there are some things we missed out on. We can also rejoice in the times in which we did obey those feelings and work toward more such times in the future.

When we fail to follow our gut, I don't believe the issue is that we feel the information we are getting is incorrect. I believe the issue is one of trust. We don't yet know how to trust our gut. We've been trained all our life to go with the calculations and computations that our mind has vetted.

A lot of time and effort has been put into the plans that we have laid out for ourselves. Besides that, it feels weird not to use your head. We are all very familiar with the expressions, "You have to use your head!" and "What were you even thinking about when you did that?"

The problem with this kind of "thinking" is that too many times we get stuck in our own head, and we become self-reliant and can't hear the wisdom coming from another source, whether God Himself or someone He chooses to use. Sometimes we can't hear God because we are too busy listening to ourselves.

To help us with this, God gave us an important reminder: *"My ways are not your ways, and My thoughts are not your thoughts."* God is saying that how He processes things is different than how we process things.

God is a Spirit, so He processes things in His Spirit. When we don't trust our gut, we process things in the natural sense, not the spiritual sense. We tend to process things in our head, not in our hearts, where our spirit is located.

God's thoughts don't come from His head; they come from His gut, the core of who He is. The essence of God is in His heart or gut. To hear God, we must listen with our gut, not our head. Look at what was said, *"He that has an ear, let him hear what the Spirit is saying."* Most everyone that was in the audience at the time this was spoken had ears, so what was the true meaning of this saying? It was to listen with the ear in your gut, aka your heart. H… EAR… T this ear!

We can only hear God with the ear in our heart. So lets begin retraining ourselves to work on listening with our H.ear.T. God has a lot of things He wants to share with you. Listen up (toward Heaven)!

This is a Thompson Truth!

NOW, WRITE YOUR TRUTH:

_____

_____

_____

_____

_____

_____

_____

_____

_____

_____

_____

_____

_____

_____

_____

_____

43

Experiential Learning

Many of us might have gained faith from an experience we had. Perhaps there was a time when we experienced something that was so profound that it literally changed our beliefs. In than one instance, we went from not believing to believing.

Some things only resonate when we can experience them. For example, Thomas said he could not believe that Jesus was alive unless he saw Him with his own two eyes. I can personally say there have been some things that I would not have believed unless I saw them for myself. These are examples of experimental learning. Perhaps you can think of something that you didn't believe in until you experienced it for yourself.

Our experiences help to determine our perspective or belief system. We believe for good, based on the good experiences we've had, and likewise with the bad. Some of us have had good experiences with God, while others have had bad experiences with Him. It my sincere prayer that, through these truths I have been sharing with you, you will begin to have some good experiences with God.

Our spirit looks through the eyes of our perspectives and experiences to comprehend and understand what we actually have faith in. Having faith without any experiences to reference it to is rare and uncommon. Some might even say that you cannot have faith without an experience. Faith takes place in us once we have learned to believe based on our experiences. One could then say that we are experientially learning.

Experientially learning is simply the process of learning through our experiences. In other words, we learn through the reflections of doing.

God is also an experiential learner. Imagine if you truly loved someone so much that you wanted to feel what they felt. That's what God is like. He wants to feel what we feel. He wants to cry when we cry, and laugh when we laugh. To do this, God had to become an experiential learner. He knows what we are going through, but He wants to know how we feel when we go through it.

In one of my previous chats, I shared the fact that God has faith in you.[16] The way God gains faith in us is through the experiences He shares with us. He wants to experience our life with us and through us, through our eyes, ears, emotions, and feelings—experientially.

Look at what a psalmist wrote:

---

16. To view the entire podcast, "The Supreme Attestation," I encourage you to visit my site: www.bentonthompsoniii.com/thompsontruths

"You keep track of all my sorrows. You have collected all my tears in your bottle. You have recorded each one in your book."

I want you to know that you are not alone in what you are going through. God wants you to know that He is right there experiencing it right along with you!

This is a Thompson Truth!

NOW, WRITE YOUR TRUTH:

_____

_____

_____

_____

_____

_____

_____

_____

_____

_____

_____

_____

_____

_____

_____

_____

44

The Supreme Attestation

When someone attests to something, they are validating it as true, authentic, and genuine. It's kind of like saying, "I will personally vouch for their credibility and trustworthiness."

Validation and accreditation are trophies that we are all constantly seeking. This begins as early as childhood, when we want to hear someone–anyone — say, "Good boy!" or "Good girl!" We have always longed for someone to value us—as a friend or lover, a person in authority, someone we esteem highly. That's why we want that degree, that title, that salary, that house, that person, that car, or whatever other symbol of achievement we think will give us that accreditation to allow someone to speak well of us.

We long for credit, credit for being a good person, a good parent, a good friend, a good mate, a good neighbor, a good child, and the list goes on and on.

Is there anyone who will attest to who we are? Is there anyone who will say we are great or at least good at something? Can or will anyone say they see the good in me? The answer is a resounding Yes! God sees the good in each of us.

Tears came to my eyes as I was writing this. I felt approved and accepted, and I pray that you feel the same from reading these words. God sees the good in you! Just allow yourself to sit in that for a moment.

Allow me to say it another way: God has faith in you! Yes, God has faith in you. He has put His faith squarely in you. Let that resonate within for a minute.

Look at this statement that was made: *"What is man, that you are so mindful of him?"* In other words, "God, what makes You have so much faith in him (or her)?" We all know that mankind doesn't have the best resume and track record.

After all, Adam and Eve were disobedient and fraternized with the enemy, Cain was a murderer, Noah got drunk and was publicly indecent, Abraham got a woman other than his wife pregnant, David was an adulterer and murderer, Rahab sold her body for money, Elijah and John Mark were deserters, Tamar slept with her father-in-law to get pregnant by him, Peter lied about Jesus, Saul (also known as Paul) participated in the execution of Christians, and Benton Thompson III, that dude, … Well, let me just say, "Thank You, Lord, for Your faith in us!" Yes, despite all that we have done, God still has faith in us! He has always had faith in us. He put His faith in you and me long before we were born. I have proof of this that I would like for you to consider.

God had so much faith in us that He wagered what mattered most to Him, His only Son, Jesus. He bet Jesus' life, that we would accept the invitation to come back into fellowship with Him, come back home to Him, come back home where we belong. Now that's some faith! Which of us, who have children, would bet our child's life on anything for any reason?

God also showed his faith in us by creating us as the only ones in His image. For no one or nothing else did He use Himself as the mold for how to make it. Only to mankind did He give His name and His likeness and image, despite knowing full well what we would do and become.

We can all be protective of our inner sanctum, our home, our personal space.

God is too. He is very particular about His temple, the place where He will reside. Still, He chose our mortal bodies as the perfect location on Earth for His Spirit, the precious Holy Spirit, to reside and dwell in.

He entrusted His likeness, His Son, and His dwelling place to us. That's faith! If you have never felt validation and accreditation before, I pray that you feel it now from God's supreme attestation!

This is a Thompson Truth!

NOW, WRITE YOUR TRUTH:

_____

_____

_____

_____

_____

_____

_____

_____

_____

_____

_____

_____

_____

_____

_____

_____

_____

easy, hit hard." That's how I hit the golf ball today.

Occasionally I win when we play a round or two together. He might say that he lets me win, but I say a win is a win. He is my mentor, friend, confidant, father figure, and oldest living sibling, my big brother Tyrone.

Tyrone has always been there for everyone in our family. When I was but a six-week-old infant, a terrible flood ravaged our neighborhood and our family. Our mother was still recovering from childbirth with me, so we were all at home. The older siblings were outside playing when the rain began to fall harder and harder. Suddenly flood waters rushed through the neighborhood, and we lost our two youngest sisters, Deborah (6) and Carol (4).

My father was attempting to transport them to safety when the flood waters swept them away. But my father was not alone; Tyrone was with him. My family was devastated. My parents had nine children in all. But on that fatal day, we were two less.

Over the years and through the trials of life Tyrone has been there for every one of us. He was the second oldest child. There are only three of us left now–Tyrone, Randolph, and myself. Tyrone has been a true blessing in my life. He is a fearless, resourceful, kind soul. He is loved by his family and friends, honored by his church, and respected in his community. I have always followed his example.

Tyrone, I appreciate all the godly counsel you have given to me my whole life. You often remind me of the wisdom that our father (Thompson Truths) shared with all of us. I appreciate all the support you give me regularly. You often call and tell me how a Thompson Truth podcast has touched your life and how you encourage others to listen. I dedicate this book to you because you have cheered me on my whole life. You even recommended that I write this book. You are the very embodiment of a Thompson Truth. Big Brother, I love you so very much! God's continued blessings on your life.